The Crypto Files

The Crypto Files

My First Year as a Crypto Investor

William Kirby

© Copyright 2023 William Kirby

All rights reserved

Cover Design by Nicki Algar

Author's Note

It came to me to write this book around Christmas 2022. The year in Crypto had been so eventful that you couldn't make it up. As a first time Crypto Investor I thought this is something I could pass on.

I intended to complete and publish this book by the end of February.

However with the demands of full time work and family life this hasn't quite happened. So the release date is a bit later than planned. However the content remains relevant and gives an account of what it's like to engage with the crypto market as a new investor.

Crypto moves so fast. That is the prices or values of cryptocurrencies and tokens as well as the news and general development in the space.

As a result there may be places in the book where I refer to the price of Bitcoin (BTC) for example at one price, yet in other places I refer to the BTC price at a different price. This just reflects when I have written (or re-written) a particular part of the book. While I've tried to avoid obvious discrepancies I have not got too stressed about making all price references correspond to a particular point in time for the whole book. Suffice to say that prices are relevant to the timeframe of writing the book, that is between end of December 2022 and May 2023.

In the same way references to dates of certain events may have been and gone within the time of writing the book as well. For example some Ethereum upgrades have come and gone in the time of writing the book.

I would have had to continually re-write the book to make it absolutely up to date and so please forgive any slight timeline discrepancies as well.

Disclaimer

The content of this book is an account of my experiences and what I have learned in my time in the crypto market so far. Please do not construe any of it as financial or investment advice in any way. I am investing with an amount that I am comfortable with and do not recommend that anyone follow my path. Everyone must make their own decisions based on their circumstances and risk tolerance.

Finally I report my journey and my learnings as a first time investor and participant in the crypto space. It's a fascinating and fast moving space with so much going on. I think I have a decent handle on things, however there may be the odd imperfection in my understanding of certain facts. I encourage anyone to do their own further research should they wish to verify any of my comments and assertions. I do not believe I have any particular biases, only opinions that I have formed in my time studying the technology and the space in general. However if there is any error or offence caused then I apologise in advance. This is certainly not my intention.

Contents

Introduction 5

Part 1: Getting Started 9

   Initial Portfolio 9

Part 2: How it Unfolded 19

   Portfolio Evolution: Bitcoin and Ethereum 19

   Running Blockchain Nodes and Earning Rewards 22

   Adventures in DeFi – Decentralised Finance 31

   Degen DeFi ! 45

   Macro Economics – Inflation, Interest rates and a Bear Market 49

   Flight to Safety (Sort of) 52

   De-leveraging of the System 53

      Terra Luna 54

      Celsius 63

      FTX 70

Summary to Part 2 76

   Evolution of my Portfolio and the De-Leveraging of the System 76

Part 3: What I Learned 83

   What a Cryptocurrency is and why it exists 83

      Blockchain Technology and the Notion of Rewards 83

      The Benefit of Bitcoin and the Reason it was Created 89

   Assessing Cryptocurrencies as an Investment 90

Tokenomics 90

Market Capitalisation (Market Cap) 95

Bitcoin – and my Relationship with it! 96

Bitcoin Market Cycles 99

Macro Economics 104

Technical Analysis of Price Charts 111

Holding Crypto for Yield is Dangerous! 115

"The Rules" 117

Part 4: The State of Crypto in 2023 121

Mixers 121

Privacy Coins 123

Central Bank Digital Currencies (CBDCs) 124

"Operation Chokepoint 2.0" 126

Positive Takes on the State of Crypto ! 129

Bitcoin Adoption 129

Bitcion Ordinals 130

Bitcoin as 'Digital Gold' 130

Wealth Transfer 131

General 'Mainstream' Adoption for Cryptocurrencies and NFTs
.... 132

NFTs 132

Crypto as an alternative Payment System 134

Summary of the State of Crypto in 2023 136

Part 5: My Strategy Moving Forward 139

My Current Portfolio 139

Strategy for 2023 and Beyond 139

Strategy for 2024 and beyond 141

Bitcoin 143

Market Top Indicators 145

Ethereum 147

Solana and Cardano 149

Flux 151

Presearch 152

Cosmos 154

Lesson from Current Bear Market 156

Summary to Crypto Files 2022 159

YouTube channels I subscribe to or have previously subscribed to (alphabetical) 161

Introduction

I've monitored Bitcoin on and off for a few years.

I looked back on my Amazon account recently and saw I bought my first book on Bitcoin in 2017.

I recall at the time that I sought some advice from a reputable computer software developer I worked closely with at the time.

I figured he'd have some insight that I would not.

"What do you know about Bitcoin?" was the first and obvious question I asked.

I recall his reply was something like - "it's an online currency used on the black market by criminals and thieves"

Basically, it's dodgy as hell, don't even think about it.

So I recall I parked my curiosity and once again periodically kept an eye on it. Probably as it came up in the news, or just as likely when I was considering how to find outsized returns somewhere.

It was then around Christmas in 2020 that I came upon an advert in the Times newspaper for a crypto exchange called Ziglu.

It was then that I gained my first exposure to the crypto market.

I saw this as a legitimate and 'safe' way to enter the crypto market. I'd previously looked online at how to invest in this thing and not really had the daring, confidence or bravery to take the risk and buy from any exchange that was advertised online.

So I bought about £250 worth of crypto - Bitcoin, Ethereum, Litecoin and XRP.

What hit me immediately in the coming days - and even hours - was the sheer volatility of these currencies.

It was like nothing I'd ever seen before. I'd watched the stock market in the past but that has nothing on the sheer volatility of crypto. I would later learn that this is due to the market cap[1] of these products.

Because the market caps in crypto were so low then it did not take much buying or selling pressure to move the price of these currencies or tokens.

Also within days of my investments, XRP was delisted from Ziglu due to a law suit that was announced in the US. (Still unresolved at the time of publishing).

So in my first weeks with 'skin in the game' I was witnessing extreme volatility and the de-listing of 1 of only 5 currencies available on the Ziglu exchange!

Welcome to Crypto!!

Over the next year (2021) I held on to a very small amount of Cardano and Litecoin on Ziglu.

I followed the crypto markets on Crypto news apps and later found all the 'resources' of information/ education available on YouTube.

Towards the end of 2021, having watched the market go bonkers all year - mainly up but also down with the summer trough, I decided to invest some more significant money.

---

[1] Market Capitalisation is the asset price multiplied by the number of assets in circulation. For example 1000 coins at $10 each would equal a market cap of $10,000

An amount that would make a financial impact if I were successful.

As you can work out, this was a classic FOMO investment at the end of a bull run. How quickly I would need to learn.

What follows is my journey from this significant investment to the end of 2022/ start of 2023.

A fascinating experience filled with education, entertainment, plenty of bruises and complete disaster for a huge amount of crypto investors.

Part 1: Getting Started

In this part I will cover my initial investments – what 'coins' I bought. Why I bought them and what my portfolio allocation was.

Initial Portfolio

Having read plenty and listened to all sorts of people on YouTube, I researched and figured out that Coinbase was a huge player as cryptocurrency exchanges go, a publicly listed company and therefore a safe place to start. This was my train of thought.

So my first move was to set up an account with Coinbase. Coinbase is an Exchange where you can buy cryptocurrencies. This would be my first real exchange where I would buy my first proper cryptocurrencies.[2] Very exciting.

So I went through the whole set up procedure with ID etc. and all of a sudden I was ready to go. It's quite straight forward and I was able to transfer some funds from my bank onto the exchange so I could trade.

As I was just getting started with investing properly in cryptocurrency I was learning a lot about what was going on in the space. I had to understand the basics of what a blockchain was and what all the different types of cryptocurrencies actually were and what was their relevance.

Initially I realised there were a plethora of use cases and 'sectors' within the Crypto sphere. The biggest and most popular cryptocurrencies are and were

---

[2] I mentioned Ziglu in the introduction – on Ziglu you could not send your Bitcoin for example to another wallet. So I did not 'own' that cryptocurrency. Rather I held a stake in some cryptocurrencies with Ziglu. On Coinbase you can actually withdraw your Bitcoin to other wallets on the blockchain.

Bitcoin and Ethereum of course. Otherwise there were all sorts of different areas.

Around November 2021 most cryptocurrencies were operating at or near new all time high prices. Which largely meant that they had all being doing very well for investors. Of course some were doing better than others.

The prominent categories I was finding at this time were as follows:

Layer 1 and Layer 2 smart contract blockchains

Gaming tokens

Metaverse tokens

DeFi protocols

Cross chain blockchain protocols

Bitcoin (!)

Music tokens

I will not go into too much detail about what each one does but below is a basic explanation of how a cryptocurrency in each sector may work.

Layer 1 blockchains (smart contract enabled) – these are known as the base layer and are their own blockchain which has its own native cryptocurrency.

They have 'smart contract' functionality, which enables transactions to be processed according to code. Applications can be built on this blockchain (think of a layer 1 blockchain as payment software). Any transactions made on an Application are settled on the layer 1 blockchain and transaction fees are paid for in the layer 1 cryptocurrency.[3]

Examples are Ethereum (currency ETH), Cardano (currency ADA) and Avalanche (currency AVAX).

Layer 2 blockchains (smart contract enabled) – these are blockchains that are built upon a layer 1 blockchain. They are their own software but rely on the layer 1 for certain features. The transactions are settled on the underlying layer 1 blockchain.

So Applications built on the layer 2 blockchain have their own token or coin, but any transactions are settled on the layer 1 blockchain that they are built on. Layer 2s are useful if the layer 1 is very large and has a lot of usage and transactions going through it. Layer 2s are known as 'Scaling Solutions', because they can perform quicker by just using the layer 1 to settle transactions rather than processing all transactions on the layer 1 blockchain itself.

For example Polygon is a layer 2 blockchain built on the layer 1 Ethereum. Polygon's cryptocurrency is MATIC. An App built on Polygon may have its own token but will pay fees in MATIC. Polygon would settle any transactions on Ethereum and pay in ETH.

Cross Chain protocols – These are blockchains that have the infrastructure to connect to multiple blockchains easily allowing people to interact with different blockchains swiftly and smoothly.

Examples are Cosmos (currency ATOM) and Polkadot (DOT).

---

[3] I expand on Smart Contracts and Applications shortly in part 2

Bitcoin – The original cryptocurrency. A layer 1 blockchain designed to process peer to peer payments. It's native currency is obviously BTC.

Gaming tokens – So there are games built using blockchain technology which allow the gamers playing the game to earn cryptocurrency. These are known as 'Play to Earn' games. I am not a gamer myself but I believe in traditional gaming you can earn tokens or 'skins' and put them to use within the game that they were earned. The concept of 'Play to Earn' (or P2E) is that a currency can be earned and then converted to actual real value (e.g. BTC or dollars) on a crypto marketplace or exchange. In this way proficient gamers can actually earn money by playing computer games.

A star example of this is Axie Infinity (token AXS). which gained enormous popularity and the token accrued great value as a result.

Metaverse tokens – The concept of the 'Metaverse' is one where people will interact in a virtual world built on the blockchain. Here value can be transferred for a myriad of everyday events but in virtual reality. It's a new concept of course which hasn't gathered much value yet but may do in the future. People have even bought virtual land in the metaverse.

Examples are Sandbox (SAND) and Decentraland (token MANA)

DeFi Protocols – These are Decentralised Finance protocols where you can lend, borrow or exchange cryptocurrency. By lending cryptocurrency you can earn interest. When you borrow cryptocurrency there will be fees and interest to pay of course.

Two examples of lending/borrowing protocols are Aave (token AAVE) or Curve (token CRV) which are built on the Ethereum blockchain.

Another example is Uniswap (token UNI), which is a decentralised exchange where you can swap between cryptocurrencies.[4]

Music tokens – These are protocols that are trying to enable artists and particularly musicians to easily earn royalties (or commissions) from their work using the blockchain to automate the royalties and remove the middle man or 'agent.'

An example is Audius (token AUDIO).

Streaming Services – These are protocols that develop a network which incentivise participants to use the blockchain for streaming services. Either to provide content to be streamed or provide bandwidth to improve the network.

Examples are Theta Network (THETA) and Render (RNDR).

There's also a whole lot more use cases and projects as well. It's pretty endless to be honest. These were what I came across as being the most investible in my opinion from the outset.

So having established these areas as areas of interest I set about putting together a portfolio which had exposure to them all. This is because simply I

---

[4] Decentralised Finance (De-Fi) - finance protocols not governed by a centralised entity and running according to code on an opensource blockchain. The DeFi theme runs throughout this book and it is very relevant to the crypto space.

didn't know what would continue to rise and what would not. There was hype around everything in crypto at this time in November / December 2021.

So my starting point was to get a slice of it all and see what happened. Looking back it is not a great investing strategy but equally it's a way to get a start. I've learned a lot since then as you will see.

So here is my initial portfolio that I put together with which sector each cryptocurrency would fall into.

Bitcoin (BTC)

Ethereum (ETH) - (Layer 1 smart Contract -DeFi)

Solana (SOL) - (Layer 1 smart Contract -DeFi)

Polygon (MATIC) - (Layer 2 smart Contract -DeFi)

Chainlink (LINK) - (an Oracle – this propogates data from on and off the blockchain)

Cosmos (ATOM) - (Cross Chain)

Enjin (ENJ) - (Gaming)

Aave (AAVE) - (DeFi – borrowing and Lending protocol)

Gala (GALA) - (Gaming)

Decentraland (MANA) – (Metaverse)
Polkadot (DOT) – (Cross Chain)

Render (RNDR) - (Streaming)

Cardano (ADA)- (Layer 1 smart Contract -DeFi)
Algorand (ALGO) - (Layer 1 smart Contract -DeFi)

Theta (THETA) - (Streaming service)

Audius (AUDIO) - (Music)

Opulous – (Music)

My allocation to the above cryptocurrencies was roughly:

10% each - Polygon, Solana, Cardano, Ethereum, Cosmos

5% each - Bitcoin, Gala, Polkadot, Chainlink, Algorand, Aave, Enjin, MANA, Theta

2/3% each - Audius, Opulous, Rendr

As you can see it was fairly spread around with many layer 1 blockchains in there. The percentage allocation would of course fluctuate daily especially due to the volatile nature of cryptocurrency.

The dominance of the Layer 1 blockchains in my portfolio is likely due to their success and prominence at the time.

The layer 1 space had been and still is very competitive. Leading upto the end of 2021 many layer 1 blockchains and their currencies had become very popular and their value had grown exponentially.

Of course this gave them lots of air time and hype. The layer 1 competitiveness is so intense because they are all competing/hoping to be one of or even *the* most prominent blockchains on which future payment systems will be built and/or integrated. The payments industry is so huge that prominence in this field would yield great rewards.

So this was my starting portfolio. I continued to learn a lot very quickly about the whole cryptocurrency space and the technology behind it. My portfolio would evolve as my education did and as the macro economic conditions of 2022 played out as well.

Part 2: **How it Unfolded**

In this part, I will discuss how my portfolio and it's allocations evolved and why over 2022.

This includes my growing understanding of the crypto space and investing in general, my discovery of ways to earn cryptocurrency and also the macro economic factors which were affecting all assets and markets throughout 2022.

I will also look at crypto-specific catastrophic events which affected the whole market.

Portfolio Evolution: Bitcoin and Ethereum

As I studied all things crypto I was learning that Bitcoin and Ethereum are comfortably the largest cryptocurrencies and widely held as the safest to invest in.

As of March 2023 they account for 60-65% of the entire Cryptocurrency market cap.

Bitcoin has a market cap of $473 billion and Ethereum has a market cap of $207 billion. That's 43% and 18% respectively of the whole market cap which sits at $1.1 trillion today.

Bitcoin was of course the first cryptocurrency and therefore has gained enormous attention and has essentially inspired all cryptocurrencies that followed, including Ethereum.

Ethereum was the first layer 1 smart contract platform and hence it's ecosystem has grown enormously and has inspired the development many other layer 1 smart contract platforms since.

Smart contracts are part of the revolutionary technology that makes Ethereum what it is. Smart contracts underpin Decentralised Finance to make it work. They are essentially code on the software of a blockchain that says 'If x condition is met then do y.' The smart contracts themselves are immutable and distributed on the decentralised network for all to see.

They are immutable because they cannot be altered once programmed and if the conditions are met then they will fulfil the required role.

They are distributed because they are on an opensource decentralised blockchain and so can be verified across the whole network.

The 'conditions' of these smart contracts can vary widely. Once the conditions are met they will trigger the desired function or transaction.

So this is what makes 'Decentralised Finance' or 'DeFi' possible. There is no need for a central party, the smart contracts can be set and relied upon to carry out their function.

Ethereum also has further reach than it's own market cap suggests. Because it was so innovative as the first layer 1 smart contract platform it has had many Decentralised Apps (Dapps) built on top of it.

Examples of Decentralised Apps are protocols such as Aave (token AAVE) and Uniswap (token UNI). Aave is a borrowing and lending protocol built upon the Ethereum blockchain. This where people lend and borrow cryptocurrency for the stated fees and interest rates. Uniswap is a Decentralised Exchange built on Ethereum. On Uniswap you can swap between cryptocurrencies without any intermediary (hence decentralised as opposed to Coinbase for example, a publicly listed central entity).

Both Aave and Uniswap accrue value to Ethereum due to some transaction fees being paid in ETH. This is because they are built on the Ethereum blockchain.

These are just 2 examples of Dapps built on Ethereum. There are thousands more. They are all creating demand and accruing value to the Ethereum ecosystem and the ETH currency.

Therefore Ethereum has that 'first mover advantage' as a smart contract blockchain. In an industry that has grown rapidly over the last decade or so, Ethereum has a 2-4 year advantage over any other layer 1 smart contract platforms such as Cardano (ADA), Solana (SOL) or Avalanche (AVAX).

So from an investing point of view Bitcoin and Ethereum are the two 'Big Daddies' of the crypto space. There is little sign of this changing in the immediate future and so for now, as a crypto investor, they are understandably the safest bets.

When building a portfolio that is relatively safe in crypto terms, these need to constitute more than a small amount. Many investors suggest upwards of 50% of a crypto portfolio should be in these two cryptocurrencies. Some say upwards of 75% of your portfolio should be in these two.

I guess it all revolves around your risk tolerance. Bitcoin and Ethereum, being larger market cap cryptocurrencies, will not move quite as wildly as some other cryptocurrencies in value. Though they are still extremely volatile assets when compared to traditional stocks or shares. They should however, in the short to medium term, be a safer guarantee of holding value with good upside potential when compared to almost any other cryptocurrencies.

Therefore based on this I shifted the emphasis of my portfolio into Ethereum particularly at first. But also after a while into Bitcoin as well.

In the first couple of months of 2022 I would mainly be buying ETH as I was building up my portfolio. Thus increasing it's percentage allocation of my overall crypto portfolio.

Running Blockchain Nodes and Earning Rewards

As my education was evolving as I explored the blockchain world, I came across ways for the average individual or investor to earn cryptocurrency rewards by running nodes on the blockchain.

Many blockchains are decentralised networks of computers (known as Nodes), which provide their computing resources to aid or secure the blockchain. In turn these computers or Nodes are rewarded for these resources or services that they provide.

The prime example of this of course is what is known as 'Mining.' This is how the Bitcoin network is secured; miners provide their resources to validate transactions on the Bitcoin blockchain, thus securing the network. The reward given is in the native cryptocurrency – Bitcoin in this case.

I will go into more detail on this concept and Bitcoin itself in Part 3.

But as you can see from the Bitcoin example, the very essence of cryptocurrency and blockchains is that the cryptocurrency is an 'incentive' or 'reward' for providing a service on a decentralised blockchain network.

The motivation in Bitcoin's case, was to provide a peer to peer payment system without any intermediary. This incentive structure created a way to maintain the network without a centralised entity. As I said, more on this in part 3.

Anyway to me, this concept is just pretty cool. To think that average Joe can earn cryptocurrency on the side for providing some computational resources. There are varying degrees of difficulty when doing this as I explain below. However, in my opinion it's another stream of income anyone can earn given some skills and the inclination to do so.

One consideration though, as an investor, which I will touch on in Part 3 as well, is that rewards are essentially inflation of the currency and if this inflation is too high as a percentage of total supply, this can devalue the currency itself.

So I went ahead and tried running nodes with 3 projects: **Presearch, Flux and Helium**

Presearch

Presearch is a decentralised web search engine – web address Presearch.com – take a look.

You can use it like any other search engine but it is protecting your privacy and not sharing or using your data in any way to deliver you the search results. It's very 'anti-Google' because of what Google does with your data and the search results. Google can essentially farm your data and use it to monetise whatever you do on Google basically.

It seems the Presearch project stems from the founder having had a bad business experience where Google essentially ruined his business by removing his website from being at the top of the search results to being so low down that no-one could find him. The story goes that he was seen as a competitor to Google and they basically nudged him aside. I haven't verified this myself but I have no reason not to believe it either.[5]

So Colin Pape and his team have created this decentralised search engine aimed at NOT doing that to people and actually providing organic results rather than tailoring it based on what it knows about you in its algorithm. In fact Presearch provides it's search results without any information of who has made the search.

---

[5]Reidhead, K (14th Sept 2022) 'How Web3 can Disrupt Google and Change the SEO Game' https://newsletter.w3academy.io/p/how-web3-can-disrupt-google-and-change-the-seo-game

The utility of nodes on this network is that they are providing computational resource to deliver search results to 'searchers' on the website. There are nodes being run worldwide and users searching worldwide as well. Presearch uses geographical routing algorithms also to reduce lag time between searches and results. So searchers in Europe for example may be serviced from a node hosted in Europe in order to quickly and efficiently provide the results.

Rewards are paid out in the PRE token every time your node helps to route a query or search result.

Now the reason I began to run a node on the Presearch network was because it was an inexpensive way to get started running a blockchain node. The project sounded good as well and furthermore it is not difficult at all to run a node.

Since then I have come to like the project more. The team are very genuine and thorough. They have weekly streams where they update you on all developments and you can ask any questions as well. I do have some questions about how it will evolve in the next couple of years. The tokenomics concern me a little. I'll cover tokenomics in the next chapter.

I started to run a few Presearch nodes on VPS hosted services and they pay me rewards every time my node provides the computational power and delivers search results to someone on the network.

To set up a node you connect to their network by basically adding some code on to a computer – either your own at home or I use VPS hosted services. VPS means a 'Virtual Private Server' where you pay a monthly fee for someone to maintain a server in a building for you. You control the server and can install what you want to on the server remotely. This is how I installed the Presearch code to set up the node. After that you just let the server run and the host company will ensure the server is powered up and maintained as necessary.

And as long as the Presearch node is connected and online and doing its job then you get paid the rewards in the PRE token.

I have found that there is little maintenance with the Presearch nodes. The VPS service I initially used was inexpensive as well. So the result was that I was partaking and contributing to a blockchain project and earning cryptocurrency rewards at a small profit. So a worthwhile venture in the short term I think. We'll see how the node running experience and the Presearch project both evolve over time.

Initially when I ran my first node you had to buy and stake 2000 PRE in order to run a node. You would be rewarded with approx. 3.5 PRE daily.

Now the collateral required has increased to 4000 PRE per node and the rewards are about 4.5 – 5 PRE per day.

The value of the PRE token when I set up my first node was around $0.20 and is now down at about $0.05. So the token price is well down with the rest of the crypto market.

I have actually experimented with moving some of my nodes from the traditional hosted VPS service onto another blockchain and cryptocurrency network called Flux recently. This reduces the VPS cost down to next to nothing. About $0.75 - $1 per month per node at the current price of Flux.

This moves nicely into the next Blockchain Node project challenge which was to run Flux Nodes on the Flux blockchain to earn the FLUX currency.

Flux

What is Flux?

I think Flux is a very interesting and impressive project.

It is a Cloud Storage service provider where people can host websites and use cloud storage among other cloud services. Basically directly aiming at Amazon Web Services and Google Cloud business. Amazon Web Services

(AWS) is the most profitable part of Amazon's business and Flux is providing the same sort of services. The quality and reliability of which time will tell.[6]

So by running a Flux Node you are giving your computational power and storage space to their network. Whereas Amazon will have several huge data centres where all of its thousands of servers are held and running 247, Flux uses the power of a decentralised network all over the world for its computational resources. Some people have nodes running at home on the Flux network. Some people have VPS servers around the world running a node on the Flux network.

It is just a different business model to the Amazon Web Services model. This decentralised Flux network built on the blockchain takes out the cost of the hardware for Flux and allows the public to provide this and earn rewards in Flux cryptocurrency for it.

All of this is giving Flux the resources it needs to power the network. Furthermore the Flux network has perpetual back-ups as well for all Apps on the network, meaning zero downtime. It runs 3 instances of every Application and if one ever drops off then another is instantly spawned to retain 3 instances constantly.

Again this, for me, is pretty awesome. Anyone, anywhere could spin up a Flux node at home and start earning Flux rewards.

If Flux does grow and take a small percentage of the AWS business, I'm sure many would think that putting rewards into people's pockets is going to be more popular than it going to Amazon. I know Amazon are excellent at what they do and business is business, but this concept just spreads wealth rather than concentrating it. To me this is very positive and it is an outstanding essence of what genuine blockchain / cryptocurrency projects can do.

---

[6] Flux website - runonflux.io

Running Flux Nodes

Now I said that anyone can spin up a Flux node ... a caveat here is that it does require some technical know-how. And this is another reason I like Flux. The minimum requirements or specifications required to run a Flux node are high. There are different tiers of nodes which get different levels of rewards, but they are all a high spec. Flux wants quality resources for its network. It is trying to allow businesses to run on Flux. It wants people to run their websites on Flux.

So for my first node I tried to install and run an entry level Flux 'Cumulus' Node on a VPS server. I didn't quite manage it. There were technical challenges that I was not quite up to yet, so I ended up paying a VPS service provider that actually hosts the server AND installs and runs it for you. And you collect the rewards in FLUX for it.

So it was cheating a bit but that's what I did. It is still helping the network, just my skills weren't there to do it myself yet.

For a Flux CUMULUS node you need to provide collateral of 1000 FLUX and the rewards are shared between all of the nodes on the Flux network. So the exact monthly reward fluctuates a little as nodes come on and off the network. However up until end January 2023 the rewards were approx. 18 Flux per month. This has recently been halved to approximately 9 Flux per month.

Flux 'Halving'

The halving of the Flux rewards is part of a programmed part of the Flux make-up called a 'Halving' event. They are programmed to happen approximately every 2 years. Bitcoin has 'Halving' events and I will discuss this with relation to Bitcoin in Part 3. Essentially it is making the cryptocurrency less inflationary and therefore aiming to maintain value over the long term. In the short term it can affect the profitability of running a node or mining for rewards. However in the medium to long term it reduces the issuance of new coins (inflation), thus creating more scarcity and reducing the amount of new Flux on the market for people to sell.

My Plans for Flux Nodes

With regards to my Flux nodes, the downturn in price in the market running a node in this way is also not profitable anymore either. You may as well just buy the Flux cryptocurrency on an exchange for the cost of paying the hosting service. Nevertheless I am continuing as I am in contract for the next couple of months with the hosting service. Not a huge loss anyway. Plus, if the price of Flux flies up in the next bull cycle, I'll end up in profit anyway if I choose to sell any.

Now one of my goals (time permitting) for 2023 is to deploy and run my own entry level Flux node at home.

I actually would like to run 2 from home.

The first one will be a Flux 'plug and play' device that are available to buy. They are a small computer you can buy that has everything programmed in. The Flux software is all installed and you just need to plug it in at home, ensuring that your internet connection speed is good enough and fast enough and link it to your Flux wallet (called Zelcore wallet) and you will start earning the rewards.

For my second node I hope to do the whole shebang myself. It will take some time and energy but it is a challenge I am looking forward to. I need to re-purpose an old machine, get the right memory and SSD on there and then install the Flux software and see if I can get it going!

I'm looking forward to the challenge. I'm not convinced I'll manage it on my own but I will give it a good effort and fall back on some contacts I have if required! The Flux community forums are an excellent source of assistance for anything you need help with.

I'm also aware that the maintenance of a Flux node is not simple either. As I explained earlier the Flux project has a high bar for the quality of it's network. So all hardware and software will need to be kept up do date to keep contributing to the network and earning the rewards.

One thing to note for running nodes is the cost of electricity. This is of course a factor to take into account. For the Flux Cumulus node, the device used for the plug and play is what's called a Raspberry Pi and does not use much electricity. I do have an individual electricity meter to monitor this when I get going. However with crypto mining on powerful machines the electricity cost is a huge factor. For nodes I'm sure it becomes an issue the higher the spec and power of the required equipment.

Helium

Helium is another interesting project.

Helium is a project trying to build up a network of 'hotspots' for an 'Internet of Things' network. Many day to day devices would benefit from an internet connection or signal to store and transmit data on a long-fi network. This would be very expensive to create the infrastructure and so Helium is facilitating this with it's decentralised network.

Such general day to day devices could be weather data collectors or vehicles which can connect to a network and feed data back where necessary. Watches are another example as well. There is a perception that the need for this long-fi network will in part be driven by a new desire to gather all of this data from our daily devices.

People buy and place Helium 'miners' in a window high up in their home or building. These Helium nodes or miners are essentially giving a signal point on the network and they interact with other miners around them to provide a better signal and enable the 'Internet of Things' network to function. This in turn generates reward for the person running the miner. So again this is the incentivisation for individuals to provide the infrastructure for a network.

If you look on Helium's global device tracker its astonishing how big the network has grown in such a small space of time.[7] This was funded by high incentives initially. However since then the rewards have been significantly reduced and the value of the Helium token has absolutely plummeted and so buying Helium miners is less incentivised and more speculative.

The lead time to get my miner was about 3-4 months. This was an early example of me just wanting to get involved with blockchain nodes . I was investing in blockchains and cryptocurrency so thought it worthwhile to actually be involved and understand what it takes and what goes on.

For the record I have never bought any Helium tokens. Just the Helium miner.

Helium has recently struck a deal with T-mobile which could produce growth and value long-term. They are also trialling the roll out of a 5G wi-fi network in the US. From what I can gather the infrastructure required for a sustainable 5G network will be immensely expensive to implement. So Helium is attempting to decentralise this and let the people provide the network.

I've read that the tokenomics of Helium have changed a lot recently to the detriment of some of the original Helium miners, so we'll see how this project plays out.

In truth I haven't delved deeply enough into the Helium project. On the surface I think this concept is really good. I think the idea of people providing required resources in return for a reward just makes sense.

Of course in general this model will have its problems and may ultimately be unsustainable in some instances. However where it can and does work I think this is potentially a very good thing.

---

[7] explorer.helium.com

Web 3.0

Presearch, Flux and Helium capture the essence of what Web 3.0 is supposed to be.

Web 1.0 is the initial version of the internet with static websites that were read only.

Web 2.0 represents the interactive internet that we have today, where we can post content ourselves. The forums for this content are maintained by centralised entities such as Google, Facebook, Twitter etc. Both the economic structure and physical structure is very centralised. Economically the big companies are profiting from the whole web 2.0 – Google, Facebook, etc. – and also the servers and resources are very centralised within their companies and networks.

Web 3.0 is supposedly a follow on version of the current internet, that will accrue value to the individual users (via cryptocurrency in theory) rather than the centralised entities that rule the roost today. So computational resources will be provided in a decentralised manner by the participants rather than a single entity. Equally decision making will be conducted in a decentralised way where participants vote on the development and evolution of projects.[8]

We'll see if this plays out but the essence of this is captured by the Flux, Presearch and Helium projects.

Adventures in DeFi – Decentralised Finance

Another area I was beginning to learn about was Decentralised Finance (DeFi) and Yield Farming.

As an investor yield is generally viewed as a good thing. Some assets bear yield, others don't. Investment property produces rent (albeit with several

---

[8] This is known specifically as 'governance' in the crypto-space

costs as well), some Stocks give dividends. In the same way cryptocurrencies can bear yields in various forms.

The most common forms of yields produced in DeFi are for **staking**, **lending** and **liquidity providing**.

<u>Staking</u>

Staking can only occur on 'Proof of Stake' blockchains. Examples of these are Solana, Cardano, Avalanche.

Staking as an investor is the act of lending your coins for someone else to 'stake' or put up as collateral in order run a validator node on the relevant blockchain to earn rewards. As the lender of those coins you will earn a significant percentage of those staking rewards.

Staking relies on a consensus mechanism called 'Proof of Stake.' For context here, different blockchains have different 'Consensus Mechanisms.' These are the mechanisms by which a blockchain network reaches agreement and validates the transactions that have been processed on it's network. It is an essential part of decentralised blockchain technology and keeps the network and it's transactions accurate and truthful.

Bitcoin uses a 'Proof of Work' consensus mechanism which I will cover in Part 3. On Proof of Work blockchains, 'miners' perform hash functions to compete to validate a block of transactions to then earn the reward.

Proof of Stake networks require people to run 'Validator Nodes' known as 'Validators', as opposed to 'miners' on a proof of work blockchain like Bitcoin.

Validator Nodes check and confirm transactions as accurate on a blockchain. These Validator Nodes have high spec requirements and the validators themselves are required to 'stake' a certain amount of the native cryptocurrency as collateral to be able to run a validator node. The stake or 'collateral' is required from the validator because they essentially stand to lose this collateral if they try to manipulate the network in anyway - for example someone trying to manipulate the transaction history of a block in their own favour. It is known as 'Slashing' if your stake is confiscated as a result of bad activity.

Therefore you can see that 'consensus mechanisms' are in place to maintain agreement on the transaction history and therefore they uphold the integrity and security of a network. On a 'Proof of Stake' network, the threat of 'slashing' is the punishment threat for anyone who tries to manipulate anything.

So to earn rewards from Staking, average investors like you or I can lend our cryptocurrency to someone who will combine it with that same currency from other people/investors and use it as collateral to run a Validator Node. The validator will earn the rewards from a particular blockchain such as Ethereum[9] for example.

An Ethereum validator is required to Stake 32 ETH as collateral in order to run a Validator Node.

I believe the rewards are approximately 5% per annum for Ethereum.

So in the example of Ethereum, a validator may own say 32 ETH themselves and therefore already run a Validator Node. However validators can stake more than 32 ETH in order to earn more rewards and also gain benefits when it comes to voting rights for any proposed Ethereum protocol changes. So when staking some extra ETH, a portion of those additional rewards will be passed onto the investor who has lent or staked their coins to the validator.

Different blockchains have different collateral requirements and different annual reward percentages. The staking rewards range from about 4% - 21% from what I have seen. Mostly in the 5% - 10% range though.

---

[9] Ethereum is actually in transition at the time of publishing to becoming a Proof of Stake blockchain. It has used a Proof of Work consensus since its inception.

Lending

Lending is fairly obvious. There's a demand for borrowing crypto – so you lend it and get the interest. Protocols like Aave facilitate this. So you may lend some Bitcoin for an interest of 2-3% per annum for example.

Liquidity Providing

Liquidity providing is a very interesting topic with many layers.

Decentralised Exchanges such as Uniswap rely on 'Liquidity Pools' to allow you to swap between cryptocurrencies efficiently.

Liquidity Pools are pools of cryptocurrencies – usually 2 currencies in a pool but sometimes more – which allow traders to make an efficient swap between the cryptocurrencies in that pool.

For example, let's say someone, Adam, has USDC[10] and wants to buy some ETH on Uniswap.

A liquidity pool has previously been created on Uniswap called ETH-USDC and Uniswap have offered investors rewards for depositing their USDC or ETH into that liquidity pool. This liquidity pool provides 'liquidity' for people on Uniswap to trade between USDC and ETH.

The pool has received deposits of both ETH and USDC and the balance of the pool is 50% ETH and 50% USDC for this example.

So Adam comes along to use 1000 USDC (equivalent to $1000) to buy ETH.

Uniswap enables this trade and accepts the USDC into the liquidity pool and gives him some ETH out of that same liquidity pool.

---

[10] USDC is a stablecoin. 1 USDC is equivalent to 1 US dollar. Essentially a crypto version of the US dollar.

The balance of the liquidity pool is now slightly more USDC than ETH. Lets say 51% USDC and 49% ETH.

Now Uniswap charges Adam a fee for making that trade. Lets say the fee was 1%. Uniswap may take 0.5% (5 USDC) of this fee for itself and give 0.5% (5 USDC) to the liquidity providers as a reward for providing liquidity to the pool.

So if you consider the amount of transactions per day on Uniswap between USDC and ETH then there are a lot of fees being earned and then split (not necessarily evenly!) between Uniswap and the Liquidity Providers.[11]

So Liquidity Providing in this way is a way to earn some yield on your cryptocurrency.

There are other quite complicated layers to understand before entering Liquidity Providing and Liquidity Pools. I feel it's a bit too heavy reading, especially at this stage in the book. Therefore I'll summarise some below and I may even follow up with a separate book and include some more detailed analysis on this.

For now though, factors are:

1) The value of the assets in Liquidity Pools may change from when you deposit to when you withdraw your funds. This can affect the value of what assets you get back upon withdrawing from the liquidity pool.

2) The trading volume (demand for this liquidity pool) will vary and this will directly affect the fees paid out to the liquidity providers. This can change daily, though is more stable with larger pools of funds and more stable assets.

---

[11] As of April 2023 Uniswap is averaging approx. $500 million in annual transaction fees on the whole platform. Data from tokenterminal.com
https://tokenterminal.com/terminal/projects/uniswap

3) The Size of the liquidity pool – i.e. the amount or value of assets deposited into the pool will change with time as new investors come in and go out. Therefore your portion of fees will fluctuate with the Pool size as well.

My experiences in Staking, Lending and Liquidity Providing

Staking

I have used staking services both on centralised exchanges such as Binance as well as on the blockchain proper with decentralised exchanges such as Cosmos Hub and Osmosis. I've earned yields such as 7% APY for Solana (SOL) and locked up my Solana for perhaps 3 months on Binance. I've had 20% APY yields for Avalanche (AVAX) on Binance, again where I've locked it up for 2-3 months at a time.

I had some LUNA locked up for approx. 10% APY as well…Later in this chapter there's a story to this!

I've also used decentralised exchanges on Cosmos to stake my Cosmos (ATOM) for 21% APY.

With staking you are of course earning more of the crypto that you hold. Which seems an obvious thing to do. You are holding it so why not use it to earn some more for not much effort? And this is generally what I have done.

However there are drawbacks:

One drawback is that it is locked up for a set period and you cannot get it back until it 'matures'. However sometimes you can redeem it early at a cost. You will generally forfeit some or all of the staking rewards in this case.

Another drawback is that if you try to redeem it early, it can be 3 or more days before you actually get your crypto back. In some cases it's 20 days or even more. In a crypto market that is very volatile, if your crypto is staked, it cannot be quickly redeemed and sold if there is a need to sell it quickly due to a market downturn or other events.

As you'll see later in this chapter I experienced this more than once in 2022!

A final drawback or risk of staking is the validator that you are giving your crypto to. What if they misbehave and have their stake slashed by the blockchain? You stand to lose all of your staked cryptocurrency.

I personally have not heard of this happening but neither have I looked for examples either. Nevertheless it is a risk. It means that you have to choose your validator carefully. There are suggestions out there of how to best select a validator to reduce this risk. The suggestions and advice is largely based on a validator's history and performance.

Ethereum Staking

I hold Ethereum but do not stake it. Below is why.

The situation around Ethereum is quite a unique one right now. Ethereum took the decision to move from a Proof of Work to a Proof of Stake blockchain.

This transition is in process right now and will take a few more months to be officially complete and make Ethereum a Proof of Stake blockchain.

The move to Proof of Stake meant that people would now be allowed to 'stake' their Ethereum *to* a validator or *as* a validator, in order to secure the blockchain and earn the staking rewards.

However a couple of years ago Ethereum decided to allow people to stake their Etheruem *during* the move to Proof of Stake which meant that the staked ETH would not be redeemable until they officially complete the move to Proof of Stake. So essentially any staked ETH was staked with an indefinite lock up period. Some people have had their ETH staked for well over a year.

There has since been the innovation of 'Liquid Staking' which has created a way of being able to trade a staked cryptocurrency and even earn some more yield on staked cryptocurrencies such as ETH. More on this later and it's one to explore further yourself as well. Interesting.

So I choose not to stake my ETH due to the lock up period and also I've not quite got comfortable with Liquid Staking yet. It's essentially a 'synthetic' asset or synthetic version of ETH. I view ETH and BTC as the most valuable cryptocurrencies and so do not wish to 'play' with them in DeFi much. Especially when it comes to synthetics or pegged versions. I just prefer to hold and secure the pure form.

The ETH example though is an extreme and unique example of a staking lock up period.[12]

Lending / Borrowing Protocols

I have not used any lending protocols to lend or borrow any crypto so nothing to report there!

Liquidity Providing

I have done some liquidity providing on a site called Beefy Finance.

Beefy Finance calls itself a Multichain Yield Optimiser. I have found the site very easy to use.

You simply choose the blockchain (aka 'chain' for short) you want to use and search the liquidity pools available on that chain. It covers a vast array of chains. It is essentially connecting with many different DeFi protocols and

---

[12] As per the Author's Note to this book, Ethereum's move to Proof of Stake is almost complete at the time of publication of this book and validators are beginning to be able to redeem their staked ETH in stages

creating a marketplace for liquidity pools to make it easy for the user to search and find one suitable.

It gives all relevant information it has on the liquidity pools so you can make an informed decision about which ones to use. Information such as the annual or daily yield, liquidity pool size also known as TVL or Total Value Locked. It also gives a guide 'Safety' score for each liquidity pool.

With regard to the 'Safety' of these pools, the main element of security risk here would be 'Smart Contract Risk' which is where the code may have an error or loophole which allows someone to hack or drain the funds from the liquidity pool. You will likely have heard of hacks in the crypto industry and it does happen. Many liquidity pools are audited by a handful of well known auditors such as Certik and Peckshield. However even some audited pools have subsequently been hacked.

Auditing is not an area I know enough about to be an expert but this covers the basics.

Another good feature of Beefy Finance is that any rewards that you get are automatically compounded daily. So if you receive 0.05% in rewards in one day, that will be added to your balance for the next day to increase your investment amount.

From my understanding this has not always been available in DeFi and still is not in many protocols. I know many times you need to manually go in and 'compound' any of your earnings as often as you can. So this auto-compounding feature is a good one as it saves a lot of time.

Fantom Liquidity Pool – FTM-TMB

By mid 2022 I had added another layer 1 smart contract platform called Fantom (FTM) to my portfolio. It was with Fantom that I first started trying out liquidity providing.

After buying some FTM, I had seen some decent yields available with Fantom when paired with a token called 'Tomb' (TMB) which was 'pegged' to the value FTM.

As I have mentioned previously, underlying factors that affect the liquidity pool are the balance of each cryptocurrency within the pool as well as the values of each cryptocurrency in the pool.

The balance of the pool was 50% TMB and 50% FTM. This means that when I entered with 400 Fantom, I would have to convert half of this into TMB and keep half in FTM, and then deposit all of this into the liquidity pool.

So if 1 FTM was worth $1 and TMB was pegged at 10 TMB to 1 FTM, then 1 TMB was worth $0.10

Therefore I would have entered 200 FTM and 2000 TMB into the liquidity pool. A 50-50 split in dollar terms.

As I have already said TMB was 'pegged' to FTM.

This means that if TMB holds it's peg to FTM, then you will get the same balance out of the liquidity pool as what you put in PLUS the yield. So if I put 200 FTM and 2000 TMB at 10% yield, I would get out 220 FTM and 2200 TMB.

So this liquidity pool was all going fine – really fine in fact. The peg held and I actually received 4% yield in the first month – yes 4% yield. That's pretty good. Almost too good to be true! There are some good yields to be earned in a crypto bull market I'm sure.

HOWEVER, then TMB completely de-pegged from FTM. This means that the 2000 TMB were now not pegged at 0.1 FTM, but they were more like 0.01 FTM! So as a result my 2000 TMB were now worth about 20 FTM.

So having put in 400 FTM (200 actual FTM and then converted 200 FTM to 2000 TMB) I would now come out with the equivalent of 220 FTM plus a bit of yield!

So this was an overall loss due to the de-pegging of TMB from FTM!

I appreciate the concept of liquidity pools is not always an easy one to grasp. I've used the figures here to help illustrate the events. The actual numbers and peg ratio was different. As I mentioned I may cover this fascinating concept in more detail another time.

Suffice to say my liquidity pool providing was supposed to turn me a profit but ended up losing me some crypto instead!

The conclusion and lesson here is not to muck around willy nilly with pegged assets! Especially a pegged asset such as TMB that has no real value and was just created to draw people into a DeFi protocol experiment.

Pionex Trading Bot

I tried an automated Trading Bot on a website called 'Pionex' for a while. Due to the volatility of crypto, trading it can be very profitable. However I do not have the time or skills to do this so thought I'd try a trading bot to see what happened.

How it works is you choose the pair that you want to trade. I chose USDT[13] and BTC – essentially bitcoin against the dollar. You deposit USDT and set up the trading bot with a price range and how you want to divide it up. For example you may choose the BTC price range $25,000 - $30,000. Divide it into 40 price points and you will have a Buy or Sell point every $200 in that range (a range of $5000 divided by 40 is every $200). Click start and just watch. If the BTC price goes out of this range then there will be no trading. You would need to re-set your parameters to a new price range.

What happened in my case was that profits would be made daily and each trade would yield between 5 and 20 cents. There were between 1 and 5

---

[13] Like USDC, USDT is a stablecoin pegged to the US dollar. Another crypto version of the US dollar.

trades a day. My holdings would be a mix of BTC and USDT. The bot was buying BTC as low as it could and then waiting for the sell price to trigger the sale of that BTC. So as a result it held onto the BTC it was waiting to sell while there was also the USDT that was originally there or that had been produced from a profitable trade.

Of course if you put in a serious amount of money then these profits become larger. The bot performance metrics extrapolated it's returns to equate to 15%-25% annual profit at the rate it was performing.

The problem I had was that the market was in a down trend and my bot was a 'long bot' – i.e. it was trading on the basis of BTC appreciating in price. So my initial range of $27,500 - $32,500 was left behind as the BTC price declined towards $20,000 range.

I did add a new range but the price went below this one as well. It was at this time when I just decided to flip most of my holdings into BTC and just hold it for safety. I was de-risking and simplifying everything. This Trading Bot was a casualty of that.

The result of this trading bot experience was that I ended up coming out with a small trading profit of less that $50 accrued over a few weeks and also I was stuck with any BTC that the bot had bought around the $27,500 level.

This didn't bother me because I was in the process of acquiring BTC anyway. Just this was purchased at a higher price point than I could have bought it for. That's just investing. If you're a long term investor then this shouldn't bother you anyway.

My take-away from this experience is that this bot is probably a good one in a bull trend, when prices are increasing. When the trend is downwards then while there are some small profits to make, you will end up losing money with a 'long-bot' which is trading on the expectation of price appreciation. This may be one to re-visit when Central Bank interest rates start to decline and liquidity comes back into the system to push asset prices upwards.[14] Other trading pairs will give more volatility and therefore more potential profits as well.

Overall the trading bot did as it said it would, just I wasn't expert at using it and the market trend was down.

GMX

After the FTM-TMB experience I learned the hard way the risks of liquidity providing and of pairing your assets, (FTM) in this case with a synthetic asset pegged to it (TMB). And also this taught me really not to 'play' with any assets that you don't really want to hold anyway. For example if Bitcoin goes down in value I can handle that because I have a long term outlook there. Whereas TMB was a short term speculation based on the promises of rewards from what turned out to be an unsustainable liquidity pool!

The only other liquidity pool of any note that I have entered and am still in as it happens is on GMX.io

This is a Decentralised Exchange (DEX for short) where people trade on leverage. I provided some ETH to a large liquidity pool which has BTC, ETH, USDC and a couple of other high quality crypto tokens.

The fees are paid to liquidity prividers from when people trade on leverage on the DEX. Often leverage traders end up losing and paying more out than they earn! So this seems a pretty good play for now and I have some ETH parked in there earning me around 15-20% in rewards. I've been in that pool for about 4 months or so now. I try to keep my ear to the ground to make sure the GMX DEX is still functioning well and a safe place to park money.

---

[14] I will discuss central bank interest rates and liquidity later in this book

So far so good. In any case I only have about 10% of my ETH holding locked up in there anyway. A lesson learned!

I do intend to exit soon and hold the pure ETH again. Essentially this liquidity pool converts your ETH into a different token for the duration of your 'investment' and so I could actually lose out if ETH jumps in price significantly while I am in this liquidity pool.

Yieldfarming.com

Yieldfarming.com was where I got the tip for the GMX protocol. I came across yieldfarming.com on a YouTube ad, clearly targeting people looking at crypto content.

So I joined their free programme called 'Beat the Banks'. They are a group of people who have being playing the crypto markets for a few years. They've all made a lot of money and lost a lot of money over the years, learned from mistakes and are now well placed to make money with liquidity providing and other such adventures in DeFi.

I've listened to some of their free programmes, training and advice and it all stacks up and makes sense to me. However they are constantly trying to funnel you into their paid-for service, which is understandable. They are feeding people expert crypto tips on how to navigate and earn in the crypto world. You have to accept that it's high risk and that you will lose sometimes, but you can mitigate losses and weight your investments in the safer plays. They talk about this a lot. I do think they genuinely are good at what they do. They play high risk with a small portion of their portfolio and are ready to get out at an instant. They know they have to be on their toes. They have their ear to the ground as well.

I suspect they want somewhere in the region of $20,000 to get on their paid programme. They are only looking for high earners/ high net-worth individuals with cash to play with. I'm not in that category. Nor do I have the time to give to this right now. Though I am very curious. It is potentially a head start in a brave new world of finance. Anyway it's too costly and too far out on the risk curve for the time I could give to it anyway.

Degen DeFi !

So Crypto around its height had all sorts of projects offering crazy yields of 1% per day, some 2% per day and then others eventually more. It was just crazy stuff.

Some people were making plenty of money on this. Clearly it was shaky and not likely to be sustainable.

Again and more out of curiosity I gave this a whirl with a very small portion of funds and sure enough as expected this went south as well!

These were known, affectionately(!) as Degen DeFi projects (short for Degenerate – i.e. ridiculously high risk!!) These were projects such as Strong Nodes and Thor Finance, Horde and a host of other such projects.

These were ponzi projects however they would actually pay out the yields promised – 1% per day etc. BUT, the payout (reward) was in their token.

So for example Thor Finance would pay in the THOR token. The problem was that due to such high inflation of 1% per day, the THOR token value would spiral down in $ value as early investors took their profits while later investors were coming in. The sell pressure on the THOR token would be so high that it would decrease its value exponentially and rapidly.

So strictly speaking the rewards were paid, but the value was decreasing and very quickly almost all gone. So any money invested was devalued as soon as the first 'investors' started to sell.

Clearly many of these projects were designed to just take money from later investors. Outright scams. However I'm sure some were designed (naively) to try to maintain some sort of honest rewards but were just unsustainable in the end.

Also just to put things in perspective as I entered my DeFi experimenting stage the crypto market was on a downturn. Prices were tumbling across stocks and crypto. So this meant that crypto and therefore these Degen projects had no more liquidity coming into them, and hence they were failing. They relied on new money coming in to prop up the value of the token to enable the rewards to hold their $ value. Of course the reason why the projects had even survived a few months was because of the general euphoria around crypto that kept new money coming in.

As soon as there is no more liquidity coming in then these 'projects' would never get enough money to keep them going.

That said, a lot of money was made by some folk as genuine early starters in these projects. Some however were out and out 'rug-pulls' which didn't last a week before the founders ran off with the money! Crypto is like the Wild West in this regard. So many people are trying to take your money in an unregulated and decentralised space!

Offers of 1% per day really should be huge red flags of course. I'm sure it will happen again though!

Yield Nodes

Yield Nodes was one such project but slightly more credible – only slightly though in all honesty. They had been giving yields of between 10 and 20% per month for about 2 years upto this point.

This was the other one I dabbled in and of course in the end this has gone to the wall as well. These were partaking in 'masternoding' – essentially just running nodes on a blockchain for the rewards, but supposedly 'masternodes' got a bigger reward. Again all was going well until liquidity dried up. It turns out that the majority of funds that Yield Nodes were holding was in their native coin Sapphire (SAPP) rather than BTC or something safer. Hence when the liquidity was drying up and less money was coming into Crypto, the value of Sapphire too tanked and the funds were worthless.

However I must add that masternoding will require a significant amount of the Sapphire token (SAPP) to be locked up in order to earn the rewards. So I can see why a lot of value was held in the SAPP token, however clearly any reserves they had were too SAPP heavy rather than BTC as it could not survive the liquidity crunch.

It was when I realised that their whole operation depended on the value of the SAPP token that the penny dropped for me. And that they were propping the price up themselves. From then instead of compounding my monthly earnings I began to withdraw them as BTC. This meant that I was able to remove some of my initial investment before the liquidity dried up. Of course right now I wish I'd pulled the whole lot out but I felt they had a bit longer before the problems came.

These guys seem really genuine though and are in the process of rebuilding. I wish them well and hope they achieve their goal.

Swapnex

This is my official badge where I was scammed! It seems everyone in Crypto has got their badge somewhere along the way. You either give up and run away from crypto or you learn and move on. Most who hang around and learn have had good results. However those who choose to leave the space are completely justified. We'll see how my experience turns out in the years to come!

This was a supposed arbitrage platform which was taking advantage of price discrepancies between different platforms. So it would buy say BTC from

Coinbase at one price and sell it on another exchange at another price for a profit. To be fair there are some genuine arbitrage bots out there which do make people money. However this was just a scam. So they were paying out between 1-3% per day and it worked for a while until there is a problem with withdrawals. From being an onlooker as many others were exploited in the crypto world in various scams this is how it all starts; withdrawal delays, then withdrawal limits and then the website just gets shut down.

What is interesting is that this was something that came up in an online chat in the yieldfarming.com network. It was not brought up by yieldfarming.com themselves, but by another participant just sharing "opportunities." The yieldfarming.com attitude was of great scepticism but that if you were already in it you had to recoup your initial investment and take it off the table and be ready to move fast. So while it was one they didn't recommend at all, it was one that if you had taken it on then it would have to be a very small portion of your portfolio and you had to be able to move quickly just in case. They'd obviously seen it all before. Wild West.

For the record the Degen-DeFi stuff is super high risk and quite honestly doomed to failure. Note to all: Avoid. It's probably off the end of the risk curve altogether!

Just buying and holding Bitcoin, Ethereum or other top 100 cryptocurrencies is volatile and risky enough. Surely!

Macro Economics – Inflation, Interest rates and a Bear Market

A poignant summary of 2022 and my first year of crypto investing is the fact that it was simply a Bear Market.

And not just any bear market, one of the most brutal for a long time. Inflation has been at a 40 year high worldwide. Interest rates have been raised quicker than at any time for years. Perhaps ever. This has crushed the crypto market. This crushed the stock market initially.[15] It is affecting the housing market as well.

The realisation finally set in around February /March time that Crypto – as well as Stocks and other markets – were actually in a genuine bear market. The trend was firmly down. ETH was not going over $20,000 as people were hoping/ expecting, BTC was not going north of $100,000.

The Federal Reserve in the US were starting interest rate hikes. I have never learned so much about macro economics than in this year, 2022.

Simply because to understand the markets and where the world economy is going, it is so important to understand what is happening and why. And also it helps you work out what is the likely outcome and in what time frame. From here you can make your investing plans.

Here is a summary of what had happened to get to this point in the economic cycle.

The C-19 pandemic had given rise to a lot of money-printing. Governments all over the world printed cash (aka quantitative easing) and gave hand outs on a record scale. This was because while businesses were hit with closure due to pandemic, people needed cash to live on. As a result businesses would now stay alive as well even though they were closed and unable to trade. The governments were giving businesses the cash to pay their

---

[15] As of May 2023 some stock indices have re-bounded very well

employees almost as normal and also funds to cover some expenses the businesses themselves would suffer. Mostly. Some industries were unlucky and did not get the funding in the same way. But in general most were completely propped up with handouts from the government.

The upshot of this was people with their normal income and time to spend it! At times though, there was nothing to do with that money! For example during lockdowns. You couldn't go out and spend your money except for on essentials such as food and healthcare.

Eventually things did slowly open up. Shops opened, certain sectors of the economy and entertainment opened and there was money sloshing everywhere. House prices rose and materials became scarce due to such high demand for home improvements.

At the same time though some folk were putting their extra cash into stocks, shares and crypto. Initially when the pandemic hit all stocks and cryptos were smashed and their values fell off a cliff, but gradually liquidity came back and was invested in stocks and cryptos as well. This meant that people picked up stocks for cheap initially and just kept going. Stock and crypto valuations just gradually soared to all time highs.

This extra cash around that had created high demand for goods was coupled with broken supply chains.

Due to the pandemic, labour forces in China and elsewhere around the world were sent home and so production was reduced to a halt before slowly re-opening. Combined with the cash that people had to spend this demand and supply shock sent prices sky high.

More money chasing the same or actually less goods (due to supply chain issues) = inflation.

As mentioned this also led to inflated stock and crypto prices.

This inflation in turn eventually led to the governments around the world trying to control it.

They did this by raising interest rates.

This of course is how inflation is historically tamed. Interest rate hikes make borrowing expensive and therefore take money out of the system. It also encourages savings because you will earn more for saving your money in a bank (in theory!). More savings equals less spending which is taking liquidity out of the system.

The crypto market is global, but of course the ubiquity of American economic influence (especially the US dollar) inevitably means that the US economy will drive much of the markets, including crypto. The US Federal Reserve started raising interest rates from March 2022, as did most other world central banks.

Pretty well every 2 months since then they have raised and raised. As I said before the interest rate has risen a record amount in such a short time.

In March 2023 it has still not yet stopped. Indeed the expectation is for another, albeit smaller rate rise in May this year. We will see.

This has removed so much liquidity from the markets creating so much downward pressure on asset prices from an investing point of view. Of course there are broader and more catastrophic effects that run through the economy. Such as unemployment and debt costs spiralling both for individuals and for companies.

As far as the context of this book goes though, crypto prices have just fallen in line – with more volatility though – with traditional indices such as the S&P 500 and the Nasdaq. So 2022 was just a year of a liquidity crunch. Some very experienced investors will have seen this and reacted accordingly, probably side-stepping the markets altogether. However others may not. Others may have held through it all.

So this is to explain basically... that my portfolio was heading south as well! With the whole of the crypto market and the stock market and most other investment vehicles.

Another factor which hit in March 2022 was the Russia-Ukraine conflict. This was a 'black-swan' event for investing terms and markets in general. It created understandable fear and removed some value from the stock market and general asset markets such as crypto. This among interest rates hikes has just served to compound the downward trend in the markets.

Flight to Safety (Sort of)

So as the markets were continuing to head downwards, prices were tumbling gradually and I was learning that Bitcoin and Ethereum would be the safest crypto assets to hold. These are the largest market caps, and therefore do not fall (or rise) at quite the same speed and amount that the other cryptocurrencies do. Value would be held better in these than in other names.

Also I was consistently learning more and more about Bitcoin and realising what it really is and that this is where the largest part of my portfolio should really be. It's just safer. Bitcoin leads the crypto market in general up to now anyway. So I continued to convert many of my cryptocurrency holdings into BTC. If I was buying anything in the mid to latter part of the year, it was BTC. If I was coming out of any cryptocurrencies, I was converting it into BTC. I'd watched the valuations of some of my altcoin holdings depreciate fast while at the same time I continued to study and learn about Bitcoin. This combination just drove me to put more into BTC.

With hindsight the best asset to hold would have of course been cash. USD to be precise. Of course no one knows when a market has fallen to its lowest point but as I look back and given the economic situation, stocks and cryptocurrencies were fairly inevitably going to fall in value. Just NOT buying anything was the best strategy in these circumstances. However we all live and learn and perhaps next time around I'll have the knowledge and discipline to just hang on and let things unwind before investing.

I will also add at this point that when you've entered Crypto at the top of the market with Bitcoin at $64,000, to all of a sudden have a price of $32,000 BTC sat in front of you, it's hard to feel that this is NOT the time to buy!

Lots of people sat on Bitcoin from previous cycles at a lower cost basis evidently have realised this and many had the patience to wait longer. They will have actually expected the price to keep falling and so creating a better buying opportunity. Until you witness this fall though I still challenge people to not jump in at say a 50% drop.

As you will see I have learned a lot about these cycles and understand them better now. We'll see how this one plays out.

De-leveraging of the System

Terra Luna, Celsius, Block-fi, Voyager ... and FTX

So in 2022 Crypto has been hit with more than just interest rate rises. Crypto is a young industry / asset class. It is of course technology as well. Therefore volatility is expected. Tech stocks are volatile, assets with low market caps are inherently volatile because it does not take much buying or selling pressure to cause big price swings.

This is of course what attracts people to Crypto as well.

As I have mentioned, before the end of 2021 was rather euphoric mode for Crypto. Almost everything was massively up, very many at or surpassing their all time high prices.

Liquidity was flowing, new people coming into the space (like me). All seemed good. However what happens when this occurs is that people take more risks that can come off with high liquidity. Also mistakes or imperfections can be papered over also.

As 2022 unfolded these dizzy heights were unwinding. As I have just noted, liquidity in general was drying up everywhere as well as in crypto.

In a downtrend with not so much new funds coming in or general liquidity, how would the space fare? Would these technologies and projects stand up to the tough circumstances that were coming?

The first implosion on the timescale was the Terra Luna / UST disaster.

Terra Luna

Terra Luna was a very interesting project which had been growing rapidly in 2021 and early 2022.

It involved a stablecoin 'UST' and the Luna (LUNA)[16] token on the Terra blockchain. It was attempting to grow a decentralised stablecoin that would underpin the crypto market.

Here's an explanation of **stablecoins** and how they work:

Stablecoins are on-chain versions of a currency, say the US Dollar. This means that they are dollars on the blockchain and therefore a cryptocurrency version of USD. These stablecoins are 'pegged' to the dollar in a way that a normal currency might peg itself to another currency, for example the US dollar.

---

[16] Since this event what was then 'LUNA' is now listed as 'LUNC' (Luna Classic) on exchanges – this original blockchain was 'forked' after this implosion. More reading for another day!

The largest stablecoins by market cap are USDC and USDT. These stablecoins are **centralised**. This means that they are issued and maintained by a central entity, as a business. In the case of USDC this is a company called Circle, USDT is issued by an organisation called Tether. These stablecoins are 'backed' by assets, which allow them to maintain the 'peg' of USDC or USDT against the traditional USD.

Because the stablecoin USDC for example is always redeemable for 1 US dollar with Circle, the peg is maintained by the promise of this. If the value goes above or below $1 then the market will take over and help re-gain it's peg. So if USDC were to drop below peg (to a value of say 98 cents), some would be bought at a discount to get it back to peg. Circle holds the equivalent amount of dollars as the amount of USDC are actually available on the blockchain.

It is vital that stablecoins are fully backed because if anyone who has USDC on-chain wants to exchange this for the traditional US Dollar, then Circle need to be able to swap the USDC for the USD. Therefore there has to be a backing of 1 to 1 in case everyone wants to redeem their USDC for USD.

So for every USDC issued onto any blockchain, there is 1 US Dollar backing this.[17]

The rest of this section about the UST /Terra Luna mechanism and the implosion of Terra Luna is based on a video by Guy at the Coin Bureau – "Terra Luna What Happened". The video is excellent. (The whole channel is excellent) It may be necessary to listen to it a couple of times to grasp it all because there is a lot going on. Go and listen to it. The below breakdown

---

[17] There are constant questions raised about the backing of the USDT stablecoin - aka Tether. There is speculation about whether it is fully backed by US dollars. However USDT has held its peg pretty seamlessly throughout the market downturn.

should be a good reference as well and may be easier than pausing and rewinding in order to understand everything![18]

I've also left out some bits in order to make it as understandable as possible for someone who may have very little experience of the crypto world at this point.

UST was an **algorithmic decentralised** stablecoin. This is in contrast to USDC, a centralised stablecoin which has the dollar reserves to back every USDC in circulation.

What is an algorithmic decentralised stablecoin?

Well it's value or 'peg' to the US Dollar is maintained by an algorithm or code if you like. The mechanism/algorithm for it's peg worked in conjunction with the 'LUNA' token on the Terra blockchain. This mechanism I will explain shortly.

However the first thing to note is that the Luna token (LUNA) was the native coin of the Terra blockchain and was used to pay transaction fees, governance and staking on the blockchain.

This is what makes UST decentralised. UST exists on a decentralised network and is maintained by the open and transparent code on the blockchain. Similarly the Terra blockchain is governed by the whole community via a decentralised voting mechanism in order to direct the development of the blockchain's development. Therefore both the code, transactions and governance mechanism is/was decentralised and not centralised.

The mechanism which was designed to make UST hold it's peg was as below.

---

[18]YouTube.com Coin Bureau (16 May 2022) 'Terra Luna & UST Collapse: What Happened? Inside Story!!' - https://www.youtube.com/watch?v=0CutSymg94I

An underpinning algorithm is that on the Terra blockchain:

$1 worth Luna can always be burned to mint 1 UST.[19]

Likewise

1 UST can always be burned to mint $1 worth Luna

Market forces then take over and incentivise traders in a way that will help maintain the peg. See explanation below:

<u>UST above peg:</u>

So if UST is valued at $1.50, you can burn $1 worth of Luna for 1 UST valued at $1.50.

You would then sell this UST for $1.50 of another stablecoin for an instant profit of $0.50

The result for you the trader is that you get a profit.

The result for UST is that you have:

1) INCREASED the supply – added new UST to circulation, which decreases the value of UST.
2) SOLD this UST immediately which also decreases the value of UST.

This helps bring the price of UST back to 'peg' – so back from $1.50 to $1 where it aims to be.

---

[19] Burning a token essentially is sending it to a non-existent address so that it can never be recovered. So it is removed from circulation. Minting a token is of course creating a new one.

The result for the LUNA token is:

Buying pressure for the Luna token – this is because you would have to buy the Luna token to burn it for the instant UST profit. Buying increases the price of the Luna token.

The token is then burned and so DECREASING the amount of Luna in circulation.

Both of these factors INCREASE the value of the Luna token. Basic supply and demand.

<u>UST below peg</u>

So the reverse of this, when UST is Under-peg:

So if UST is valued at $0.50, you can burn 1 UST, to mint $1 worth of Luna.

So you would buy 2 x UST for $1. Redeem this for $2 worth of Luna on the Terra blockchain.

You would then sell this Luna for an instant profit.

The result for you the trader is that you get a profit.

The result for UST is that you have:

1) DECREASED the supply – taken UST out of circulation, which increases the value of UST.
2) BOUGHT UST in the first place to trade for Luna – this increases demand/buying pressure for UST thus increasing the price

This helps bring the price of UST back to 'peg' – so back from $0.50 to $1 where it aims to be.

The result for the LUNA token is:

Increased the supply of the Luna token – this is because you are creating new Luna tokens when you burn UST for Luna. Increased supply will make the Luna less valuable as there is more in circulation.

The Luna is then sold for the instant profit, thus Decreasing the value of the Luna token.

So there you have it a **Decentralised algorithmic stablecoin** ! When learning about LUNA it took me several attempts to understand this concept completely. So please re-read and refer to the video referenced earlier on!

<u>Anchor Protocol</u>

So UST was becoming a very popular stablecoin. This was in part driven by a DeFi protocol called 'Anchor protocol'

Anchor protocol was giving a 20% annual yield if you deposited UST into the Anchor protocol. So as you can imagine this is very attractive on it's own.

When the crypto market is on a downtrend like it was in 2022, asset prices are generally falling. Everywhere. All crypto prices were falling too.

When asset prices are falling stablecoins are an attractive place to park your money because, assuming they can hold peg (!) then your money is not losing value like say Bitcoin was at this time.

So couple this with a 20% incentive on Anchor protocol to hold UST and deposit it into Anchor protocol and you have significant demand for UST. So the growth of UST was huge and it reached a market cap of $19 billion in the end.

Approx 80% of the UST in circulation was in Anchor Protocol.

This market cap was also driven by the general growth in popularity of UST across many DeFi protocols. The demand for UST became so high at times that it got above peg which created burn pressure on the Luna token, subsequently driving up the price of Luna as well.

So Luna and UST really were spreading like wildfire among crypto DeFi protocols and were being widely held by investors and members of the crypto community. A lot of people were holding the Luna token (including myself) and a lot of people were using Anchor protocol (not me). UST got to a market cap of $19 billion and Luna got to a $40 billion market cap. So that's a significant amount of investment and value locked in these 2 tokens.

Luna Foundation Guard and maintaining the peg of UST

Another piece of the puzzle in the Terra Luna collapse and general market implosion that followed was the activities of the Luna Foundation Guard or LFG for short.

The LFG was created in Singapore as a non-profit organization to help grow the Terra ecosystem.

There had been a scare in 2021 where UST had lost its peg briefly and this had alarmed the LFG to the extent that they were building up a reserve with the intention of partly backing UST with an asset so that in case of an emergency de-pegging, they would be able to re-store it's peg by buying UST up with the assets in this treasury.

They were planning to back it initially with around $3-4bn worth of BTC to equate to 20% of the market cap of UST.

They chose Bitcoin as the asset and they had been heavily buying BTC to keep on hand in case of a serious de-peg.

This is relevant in the collapse as you will see.

Collapse

In early May 2022 UST lost its peg. And this very quickly led to an implosion for both UST, Terra Luna, Bitcoin and the whole crypto market.

Here's briefly how it happened.

Terra Labs[20] withdrew a huge amount of UST from a DeFi protocol called Curve Finance to move it to another protocol.

At the same time an unknown entity also sold $85 million worth of UST for $85 million worth USDC on Curve Finance.

This pushed UST off its peg – below peg due to this huge sell pressure.

This was at a time when crypto prices were coming down with the general down trend in the markets. Therefore UST holders were cautious and so they also started selling UST as a precaution due to the loss of peg. About $9 billion of the $14 billion held on Anchor protocol was withdrawn within the first 48 hours of the de-peg. Of course this withdrawn UST was then sold/exchanged for other stablecoins such as USDC or USDT for example

This in turn kept pushing UST further from its peg.

Of course the mechanism to regain a below peg UST is to burn it to produce Luna and then profit from selling the Luna.

---

[20] Terraform Labs were the founding technology company behind Terra Luna, UST and the Luna ecosystem

The problem was... with prices already coming down in the market in general, the buying demand for Luna was not high, plus all the sell pressure now coming along as people were trying to sell the Luna for a profit meant that Luna essentially would keep crashing down in price:

Increase in creation of Luna due to burning UST to get Luna for a profit

PLUS

Decreasing demand for Luna due to market conditions

EQUALS downward price spiral.

As Guy from CoinBureau puts it "UST is (was) fundamentally a representation of the potential sell pressure on Luna"

If UST's market cap is larger than the market cap of Luna, then Luna cannot absorb the sell pressure from UST. And so the value will spiral down towards zero.

A Death Spiral that can't be stopped.

Meanwhile the LFG were trying to maintain the peg of UST by selling all the Bitcoin it had amassed for this such event and then buying UST with it to prop up the price.

But this was to no avail. 80,000 BTC were sold off and all this served to do was to put huge pressure on the BTC price which in turn brought the whole crypto market down with it.

In total $40 billion of value was wiped off UST and Terra Luna within a week. Also the general contagion across the crypto markets and DeFi protocols meant more value was lost.

In all a complete disaster.

BTC price went from approx. $36,000 down to approx. $30,000

UST went from $1 to a few cents

Luna went from approx. $80 to approx. $2

I managed to sell what Luna I had at about $15 a piece.

I had some staked so could not access this to sell. So by the time I unstaked this Luna it was worthless. Again these are the risks of staking. You can't access your funds quickly. Haven't I learned this the hard way! However I would add that staking is probably sensible to do only with a portion of your holding in case something like this does happen!

Celsius[21]

Celsius is a centralised platform where people could deposit their crypto to earn yield or even borrow against it.

The yield would be generated if you either lent your crypto, staked it or just held it there like a savings account.

Celsius would generate yield for you by lending it out to people and institutions. It would be staked or used in DeFi protocols to earn yield as well.

---

[21] YouTube.com Coin Bureau (23 June 2022) 'What REALLY Happened With Celsius?! What We Know!!' - https://www.youtube.com/watch?v=_ndb5y9nsLg
Again I have used Coin Bureau's explanation of events to relay what happened with the Celsius debacle. I make no apology for this – but of course acknowledge and thank Guy for his coverage of the topic. Coin Bureau's coverage on this and many topics is the best and I couldn't possibly improve on it. I think the detail of the events is relevant to this book. Hence the need to include the full version of events.

Essentially this is how a bank operates but in the traditional finance world. You deposit your money and they re-purpose it for lending or perhaps trading with it.

Banks are required to hold a % of all deposited funds in cash and the rest they are permitted to lend or trade in order to earn from it. This is known as 'Fractional Reserve Banking.'[22]

Celsius however are/were doing this in crypto which is of course much more volatile and less regulated than the traditional markets. A lot riskier. Hence the higher yields.

Though I'm sure Celsius would have argued that they simply gave more of their yield to the customer, whereas a bank would take more profit for themselves and give less to the person depositing their funds!

It seems Celsius were hit with a couple of consequences from these risky crypto investments in 2021. Firstly the keys to some of their ETH was lost and therefore this was unretrievable.[23] Also a DeFi hack on a protocol where they had deposited some funds also cost them some money.

---

[22] As of March 2023 Fractional Reserve Banking in the US especially has been quite exposed by the rapid interest rate hikes in the US. Banks are potentially insolvent due to the rapid change in value of the bonds they are holding. There is no problem unless they need to redeem those bonds early!
[23] Private keys are the 'keys' or pass phrase to access a wallet holding cryptocurrency on a blockchain. A string of words which give you access to your crypto. If this is lost then the crypto is unretrievable until the keys are found!

In 2022 however the major problem came with US regulators as well as stETH.

US Regulators

In short, Celsius was under investigation by the SEC[24] due to the high yields that it was offering it's customers.

In the end Celsius agreed to only offer its services to Accredited Investors and not the general public. Accredited Investors are people with assets or income over a certain amount, or people within the financial sector. A quick google search says someone with income of over $200,000 per annum for example.

This meant that a lot of investors withdrew their crypto from the platform because they were no longer allowed to use the service.

Of course losing such a large amount of customers would hurt any business.

Staked ETH (stETH) and Proof of Work / Proof of Stake

You will recall that I have previously outlined the unique situation around Proof of Work, Proof of Stake and Ethereum Staking at present. Here's a quick recap.

A few years ago Ethereum took the decision to move to a 'Proof of Stake' consensus mechanism from a 'Proof of Work' consensus mechanism.

Essentially this means that transactions used to be verified by miners checking the validity of transactions in each block and then add them to the blockchain. The miners are thus coming to a consensus that the transactions

---

[24] You will recall this is the US Securities and Exchange Commission who have an ongoing case against XRP

are correct and valid. Hence 'Proof of Work is a 'Consensus Mechanism.' The result is that the miner is then rewarded in ETH.

Ethereum is transitioning from 'Proof of Work' to 'Proof of Stake.' However as it stands there are a few more stages to go through to make this transition complete. That is for further reading and for another day!

Proof of stake blockchains, instead of requiring 'Miners', require 'Validators' to hold collateral and in the case of Ethereum, at least 32 ETH (about $45000 today) and stake them in order to qualify to be able to verify transactions in return for 'Staking Rewards' in the form of ETH.

So 'Proof of Work' and 'Proof of Stake' are known as Consensus Mechanisms which are a way a blockchain meets 'Consensus' i.e. agrees and confirms that the transactions in a block are correct and untampered with. The incentive to validate these transactions is the reward in the currency of the blockchain; so BTC on the Bitcoin blockchain and ETH on the Ethereum blockchain.

Ethereum staking

As I have mentioned if you hold ETH, you can 'Stake it' by lending it to a validator, who will stake ETH as a validator and earn rewards for validating transactions. In this way you don't need to own 32 ETH to be able to earn a yield on your ETH asset. You simply lend your ETH to a validator to do this for you.

In the case of Ethereum because it is not yet fully a proof of stake blockchain, the Ethereum foundation voted to allow people to stake their ETH long in advance but that it would not be redeemable until a later stage in the transition over to 'Proof of Stake'. A key stage is due to happen in around March 2023.

Therefore when you stake your ETH you are given stETH which is like a receipt that says 'you have staked ETH'

Someone then came up with the idea that this stETH token can actually be traded and then earn its own yield in DeFi protocols.

The value of stETH is pegged to ETH. It essentially represents ETH plus staking rewards for the owner.

Liquid Staking

So now not only can you 'Stake' ETH to earn a yield. You can now use the stETH as its own token in DeFi protocols.

This is known as 'Liquid Staking':

The '**Staking**' part - Your ETH is staked

The '**Liquid**' part – You can use this stETH as a liquid asset that has value and trade it or use it to earn yield in DeFi Protocols.

It is not locked away and just staked. It is still useable. Liquid.

It is risk upon risk basically. However it can be done in a less risky way. It reminds me a bit if the financial crisis in 2008 when complex derivatives caused huge issues within the global financial system.

Back to Celsius

So Celsius was staking ETH and using stETH in DeFi protocols as a way of earning the yield it needed to pay out the high interest rates to its customers.

Then... stETH lost it's peg !! Bloody pegs! Pegged assets are the scourge of 2022.

Now stETH losing it's peg is not the end of the world if you don't need to redeem it. However Celsius had borrowed against stETH in DeFi.

That's right.

They had put stETH – a pegged asset – up as collateral and borrowed against it.

So of course when the collateral, stETH, loses its value, the lending protocol does not have the collateral it needs to cover the loan that Celsius owes and therefore needs more money from Celsius to maintain the loan.

Put simply using random figures as an example:

Celsius put up $1 million worth of stETH to borrow $500,000

The value of the stETH collateral drops to $750,000

The lending protocal requires another say $250,000 or else it will liquidate (confiscate) the stETH collateral.

This is all agreed in advance of course with Celsius.

So now we have risk on risk.

Staking (risk) and liquid staking in DeFi (risk), pegged asset used as collateral for a loan (risk)

OMFG

Then of course ...

Word that Celsius may have a solvency problem got out and people started trying to withdraw their assets – including ETH.

Of course, all of the ETH was not even there! Some of it was now 'stETH' and was locked up and being used as collateral and potentially liquidated.

Next thing Celsius pauses withdrawals. People cannot take their money out.

Eventually Celsius filed for bankruptcy and the situation is still ongoing.

According to some recent news there is optimism that people will get some of their assets back and hopefully all of them. Who knows.

I'm not completely up to date on the latest news. I was not invested here.

There have been at least 2 other such centralised exchanges that offered yield on your crypto that have also had financial troubles as well. These are BlockFI and Voyager.

From what I understand they are similar in that they are centralised entities offering to trade crypto or provide yield generated by lending crypto and re-purposing it in other ways.

I'm not certain how each one operated exactly. But I believe they were of similar modus operandi.

Both platforms halted withdrawals and had solvency issues. Again denying their users the access to their crypto.

Again this Celsius episode is in part created by the de-leveraging in the system. As liquidity dries up any cracks are much harder to paper over.

While Celsius, and perhaps Blockfi and Voyager as well, are/were not necessarily ponzi schems, they require liquidity within the crypto industry to be able to generate the yields that they had committed to.

They could also have been hit in the UST–Terra Luna debacle as well. These are just the risks of DeFi as a nascent industry and a 'live-experiment' as I have heard crypto labelled as.

Certainly these events – Terra Luna, Celsius, BlockFI, Voyager were all in part caused by liquidity drying up and the process of de-leveraging, yet these blow ups were spiralling the liquidity crash further.

This is because on the back of such events, people would naturally remove their funds out of crypto altogether for safety, which in turn makes less liquidity and so on.

So this has been a pretty hard time for the crypto industry. Of course it is partially self-inflicted due to a blown up experiment of Terra Luna and some centralised lending platforms leveraging too far in a downward trending market.

The downtrend was initially created by the macro effect of tightening of liquidity due to interest rate hikes.

FTX

And then once the above had largely subsided over a few months we had the FTX saga in November 2022.

Of course this investigation is on-going and much will be revealed as time goes on. However this was yet another catastrophe for the crypto industry.

There are accusations of absolute fraud. We will see. It does not look good at all.

FTX was an exchange where you could buy crypto (and stocks as well I believe). A centralised exchange – again, ran by people and not code like a Decentralised Exchange (or DEX).

This FTX episode unfolded in early November and was remarkable to witness. Absolutely devastating again for all users with funds on the platform. Truly awful.

The day it all hit the fan, I recall arriving home slightly early and watching the price of crypto just cascade down. It was incredible to watch. By this time - a year into my crypto investing journey and not just any year … 2022 - I was by now rather numb to this cascade in prices. I'd witnessed the cascade down after Terra Luna and the gradual fall in prices all year. Another tumble was not new to me. The circumstances were though.

I was very fortunate not to have used FTX and so had no funds locked up. Therefore I watched as a spectator. I watched Bitcoin go from about $21,000 to about $15,500 in the space of what seemed like 20 minutes.

I wasn't at this point fully aware of the implications but was both desensitized to the price movement somewhat, now I was used to the volatility, yet also I was slightly fearful all the same. How low was this going? What would the outcome be?

On the face of it, it seems that FTX was using customer crypto deposits for it's own, or the owners' liquidity as well as for trading purposes rather than just holding the deposits on behalf of the customers. So if someone was holding say $1000 worth of BTC on the platform, this BTC was not safe in a wallet for withdrawal at any minute by the customer. It was in fact potentially not even there and was being 're-purposed' and perhaps even traded/'invested' by FTX or Alameda Research, a trading company related to FTX.[25]

It was a Coin Desk article[26] that raised the alarm on FTX and Alameda on November 2nd 2022. The article reported that Alameda Research had on its balance sheet an enormous amount of the FTT token, which is a token created by FTX for use on it's own platform. The idea was that traders would buy FTT and pay their trading fees in FTT to get a reduction in the price of these trading fees.

So essentially this FTT token had very little utility and FTX had the ability to print it out of thin air as Coin Desk reported.

Alameda was showing $3.66 billion of 'unlocked FTT'

The 3rd largest asset on its balance sheet was $2.16 billion of 'FTT Collateral'

There were liabilities of $292 million worth FTT as well.

Alameda was showing approximately $14.6 billion in total assets. As you can see almost half of this was in a token that could be produced on demand - FTT. Also the FTT token was being used to collateralise borrowing as well.

So FTX, Alameda and the FTT token were instantly exposed with the revelations in this article.

A large player in the space, Binance, then announced that it would be selling around $500 million worth of the FTT token on to the market as a process of

---

[25] Alameda Research is / was a trading company owned by the same owner as FTX – Sam Bankman-Fried. Alameda traded cryptocurrency with leverage.
[26] Allison, I (2nd Nov 2022) CoinDesk 'Divisions in Sam Bankman-Fried's Crypto Empire Blur on His Trading Titan Alameda's Balance Sheet'
https://www.coindesk.com/business/2022/11/02/divisions-in-sam-bankman-frieds-crypto-empire-blur-on-his-trading-titan-alamedas-balance-sheet/

'de-risking' it's exposure to FTT. Binance was an early investor in FTX and was holding this amount of FTT as part of it's historic investment in FTX.

The threat of the sale of this significant amount of FTT, coupled with the Coin Desk revelations raised alarm bells across the board and caused a huge sell pressure on the FTT Token. It also created huge concern about the liquidity of FTX and so everyone tried to withdraw their funds from the exchange.

Of course the funds were not all there.

The value of the FTT token fell from approx. $25 to $4 very rapidly.

FTX were using the FTT token as collateral for loans.

So when the FTT token value fell... the collateral would have gone. The loans would be called in and well.. they couldn't cover this. FTX filed for bankruptcy within a week or so. And apart from a few who withdrew early enough, everyone who had funds on the platform could not access them – much of them were simply not there.

Again the market was in a spin. In the following days it seems any tokens that FTX were holding plenty of as an investor themselves were just dumped on the market. Most notable here was Solana (SOL).

FTX were a heavy investor in Solana. They were holding a lot of the SOL token and subsequently at the time that FTX was being exposed to be insolvent in early November, they just sold out of their position which sent the price of SOL from about $35 to $12 within hours.

Again I watched this in disbelief.

I was holding Solana. Mine was staked, and therefore inaccessible to me. I did redeem my Solana in case I wanted to sell it but it can take a few days to un-stake your crypto. (Here we go again ... same lesson as with LUNA!) I knew this before staking but of course didn't expect this scenario!

I was ready to sell but of course I couldn't. I flipped and flopped over the next few days and once my Solana was released I finally had the option to sell.

I had been watching the Solana price of course. The strange thing about crypto and probably any investing – is that an asset price can change on news when nothing actually changes about the crypto protocol or the business you are investing in. The technology stays the same. It did the same as it did a week ago, yet the price falls. Of course in this case there was immense sell pressure from FTX. So everyone else sold as well (as I was prepared to do) – I suppose in case it went to zero. Or perhaps so you could buy back at a cheaper price. Instances of both I expect.

Incidentally a week before the FTX saga unfolded, Solana had an event called 'Breakpoint' in Portugal where they showcased a validator on the Devnet (not a live validator – but one for testing or development) which could demonstrate transaction speeds of around 1 million TPS (transactions per second). This is very fast.

Solana makes no secret of the fact that it wants to disrupt traditional payment rails. Transaction speeds anywhere near this number, even on a Devnet, help to showcase what it could potentially do. This is just an example of the strides that Solana and some other blockchain projects are making.

Nevertheless the point here is that one week Solana showcases that is evolving well and pushing on with it's development yet a week later the price of it's token completely dumped due to external factors out of it's control.

So anyway after flipping and flopping about whether to sell my Solana I hodled on. In fact when it subsequently dipped down to $9 I bought some more! Foolish or good move ..? Time will tell. After a huge pump it is currently around $23. So far so good but this is crypto. The Wild West. Expect anything.

Warren Buffet is quoted as having once said – 'Be greedy when others are fearful. Be fearful when others are greedy.'

I guess buying Solana at $9 at this moment epitomises this. By the way Warren Buffet hates Bitcoin and crypto!

The widely used crypto term 'HODL" I have learned means 'Hold On for Dear Life'. I must say this was never truer than holding on during the FTX crash. I can now relate to why and how this phrase came about – if that is indeed it's true origin. I can only imagine the previous crashes of Bitcoin as it's grown and grown. I've listened to many experienced folk/investors in the industry and looked at the old price charts and can only sort of relate to the emotion of watching these drawdowns.

Nevertheless in November 2022 I learned how it felt to HODL and not to sell. Perhaps I'll see worse in the months to come. Perhaps I'll capitulate and sell next time. We will see.

Summary to Part 2
Evolution of my Portfolio and the De-Leveraging of the System

Portfolio

So in summary my portfiolio had fallen in value. A lot.

It has become significantly more BTC heavy. And ETH. This was in part due to my continuing education and in part due to the macro economic climate of interest rate hikes slowing liquidity which led me to hold safer assets.

BTC and ETH have the largest market caps by far. As such they are the safest for 2 reasons:

Firstly because they have a higher market cap they require more buying or selling to 'move' their price.

Secondly they are also the safest because they have been around longest and are tried and tested in terms of what they are and what they do within the crypto industry.

Because they are the safest they are also likely to have less out flows in a downtrend and more in-flows in an uptrend. While they will not fly up as quickly as other smaller caps perhaps, they should be less volatile and a safer store of value.

I had flipped a lot of my holdings into ETH and BTC and, as I said before, if I was buying, I was buying BTC mainly and some ETH.

Two obvious exceptions to this were Flux and Presearch. I took to these mainly to get involved in Node operating as I have explained. So they certainly qualify as investments and I am optimistic for them both as projects. However the main driver for these investments was just to partake in the blockchain networks and earn some more crypto for doing so. They both seemed good opportunities to do this. I'm happy with the projects and the node operating has been exactly what I wanted to achieve.

I moved in and out of Fantom as well during the year. This has great credentials as a layer one blockchain and of course I did engage with Liquidity Providing on the Fantom blockchain. So this was a worthwhile experience.

However Fantom was a casualty of my 'Flight to Safety' decision to convert most of my crypto into BTC as the market has been in freefall.

Of course this freefall was in part due to the tightening of global liquidity as interest rates were rising, and also it was in part due to the blow-ups in the crypto space that I have just outlined.

Terra Luna

Terra Luna was a failed experiment. There are suggestions of some foul play that contributed to this collapse. I have not mentioned this and will leave this for you to follow up on. Either way the algorithm and strategy was not robust enough to navigate the stresses needed to become the decentralised stablecoin that it was trying to be.

Bad actors or not, technology needs to be tested to it's limit to determine how robust it is and whether it will cut the mustard when it comes to do what it intends to do. Terra Luna failed.

I am in no way criticising the people at Terra Luna or anyone in the project. It was almost a genius invention. A huge portion of the crypto industry were backing the project and indeed they were invested. The developers and strategists at Terra were brilliant. Almost genius.

This kind of technological experiment is quite amazing and serves to advance technology in general. However, quite a big BUT has to be that the repercussions were devastating to many people.

Assuming there was no malice from the Terra team in any way, they have inadvertently caused some grave heartache and financial ruin for many people.

Were Terra irresponsible? Did they consider the potential fallout of a de-pegging ? Guy at the CoinBureau suggests the decision to back the stablecoin with BTC was due to a sudden realisation that there was a new de-pegging risk that had been uncovered.

If the Terra team were to go back now would they hold their horses and try to wind down the project because the risk was too high of this de-peg? And also consider the potential ensuing financial ruin for some people?

Were they so focused on pushing forward with their project and did not consider this carefully enough?

Who knows.

The playground of crypto is dangerous because of the financial investment that many people off the street make. Including me.[27]

It is a risk-reward play. There are some rules that a crypto OG who I subscribe to has written that I find very relevant in this instance. I'll write them later on.

<u>Crypto is Experimental</u>

Make no mistake crypto is still experimental and not yet mature. Funds can go in the blink of an eye. Unexpected by many.

---

[27] This is partially why the SEC and other regulators have crypto in their sights. Crypto is akin to gambling. Unqualified investors in an unregulated space is dangerous. Inevitably people will trade on emotion instead of rationalising information. Of course Pro traders are not perfect either. However they are trained to mitigate risk and damage. That said 'high net worth' individuals, who the SEC may class as eligible to trade securities, would potentially just gamble as well but on a bigger scale.

Many crypto projects put out 'bug-bounties' for hackers to try to hack them. This is to deliberately test them to find weaknesses. This is for 2 reasons:

1) They want to improve their protocol and become a better product

2) They would rather pay a smaller but still substantial reward for someone to hack their protocol than a criminal and genuine hacker to eventually hack it and hold them to ransom for whatever amount they want. And perhaps this would even destroy their protocol altogether.

The protocols themselves are aware that they are not necessarily at full speed yet. The technology is moving so fast.

Celsius, Voyager, BlockFi and FTX

This is a story of Centralised platforms exposing themselves to the risks of the crypto market with other people's funds. To get high yields on platforms such as Celsius, people had to be aware that Celsius were 'investing' funds elsewhere in order to do this. The risks must have been suspected if not known altogether.

A huge ethos of crypto is Decentralisation. Satoshi Nakamoto clearly stated that Bitcoin was created as a peer to peer network to remove the need for a centralised entity. He/she/they referenced the financial crisis in the Bitcoin genesis block, the very first block on the Bitcoin blockchain. This has caught on in the Crypto world. It underpins the ethos and why a lot of people came in to the space and many people truly believe in this.

So in the crypto world, when a centralised platform or exchange such as Celsius or FTX has the problems that they had, this justifies the decentralisation narrative even further.

Decentralised finance is a host of protocols with opensource code. It is coded that if 'x' condition is met then 'y' will happen.

If you deposit x amount of funds at a rate of say 0.1% per day then the smart contract will just pay you out.

To be fair this has just chugged along while centralised entities have imploded. This supports this decentralisation narrative.

The funds for these decentralised protocols are held in wallets on the blockchain for all to see.

Yes there are risks in DeFi – hacks happen, often on bridges as I understand when people are bridging funds from one blockchain to another. And also when people don't protect their private keys well enough.[28] There are also genuine code hacks.

As I said the code for these protocols is opensource. Thus it can be audited before you deposit your crypto into a DeFi protocol. Pretty handy if you understand the coding that is used. I certainly think that the value of someone who understands this code can be invaluable when investing in DeFi.

Also in DeFi there are 'pegged assets' - you will receive greater yield on these sometimes because of the extra risk. There are risks of asset prices plummeting while you are locked in a DeFi protocol. However these are risks that you can learn before you enter into DeFi.

I have learned a lot after having tried a lot over the last year. Fortunately I've tested with a sensible amount each time.

---

[28] Private keys are the 'keys' or pass phrase to access your own private wallet on a blockchain. A string of words which give you access to your crypto. It is known as 'self-custody' when you keep your crypto yourself rather than on an Exchange.

So while Celsius and the likes and FTX are a HUGE blackeye for the space as a whole, perhaps it actually champions Decentralised Finance and Bitcoin as a peer to peer decentralised payment network. Who knows where it will go.

Part 3: What I Learned

In this section I will outline a lot of what I have learned over the past year as a Crypto Investor. This will include elements of the technology, investing, macro economics and other lessons.

What a Cryptocurrency is and why it exists

One of the first things I had to learn was how to assess the fundamentals of a cryptocurrency. To begin this I need to go back a step and lay out the very basics of what cryptocurrency is and why it exists.

Cryptocurrency uses asymmetric cryptography to secure wallets on the blockchain. Essentially this means that a 'public key' and a 'private key' are required to be able to access a wallet and then send any value (cryptocurrency) on a network. The asymmetric cryptography of requiring 2 different 'keys' are why it comes to be known as 'cryptocurrency'

Blockchain Technology and the Notion of Rewards

Blockchain technology is what underpins Cryptocurrency. I am going to use the example of Bitcoin to demonstrate how a blockchain works and how and why rewards are created.

Bitcoin is a blockchain.

The Bitcoin currency (e.g. 1 BTC) is created as a reward for when a 'miner' gives computational power to the blockchain network to help verify any transactions that have been sent on the network.

To use an example, someone sends some Bitcoin from wallet 'a' to wallet 'b.' The computers running the Bitcoin software (aka 'miners' and 'nodes') verify this and any other transactions as a true record of what happened. Once these transactions are agreed upon and confirmed as an accurate record, the block is added to the blockchain by miners. The miners are then rewarded for this work in newly created Bitcoin and the process begins again with any new transactions going into the next 'block.'

So as you can see the 'reward' is Bitcoin (BTC) being given to the miners in return for the miners running the software and confirming the transactions on the network.

Another way to look at this is that Bitcoin is an 'Incentive' for computers (or miners) to contribute to the blockchain network in order to confirm the validity of the transactions on the network. This is a very important concept within Bitcoin and also within what has come to be known as cryptocurrency in general. To create a decentralised network of many computers, the network needs to be incentivised to keep going. Payment or 'rewards' are this very incentive.

So in essence Cryptocurrencies are a reward for providing a service or computational resource to a blockchain network! That is the value creation.

<u>What are the benefits of having a Blockchain Network and Reward system?</u>

As we have just covered, a blockchain network is a network of computers that run the software of that blockchain (e.g. Bitcoin) and provide the necessary computational resource to that blockchain.

Decentralised Network

The perceived benefit for Bitcoin on a blockchain and the reason it was created was to provide a form of digital money that is decentralised. I.e. not controlled by any one individual, any one bank /country/ government.

Digital money had not previously existed without a 'middle-man' – i.e. bank

This was because previous attempts had not solved the 'doublespend' problem and so a central authority (e.g. a bank) had always been required to keep the ledger of who sent money to whom.[29]

To solve the 'doublespend problem' is to avoid the same 'digital coin' being paid out twice to different parties. To avoid this we traditionally have banks keeping ledgers so that they can check that the exact $1 that was sent from Alice to Bob, was not also sent to Charlie at the same time. Clearly, in order to function correctly a digital currency can not have this potential 'doublespend' event as a possibility.

On the Bitcoin network, the thousands of mining computers are each giving their service to the Bitcoin blockchain and the common 'consensus' is what confirms that all transactions and values are correct. Nothing on the network can be manipulated. No coin can be 'doublespent' because of this. If there was a problem someone would flag it up and people (i.e. miners and nodes) would agree to reject the transaction or the block of transactions.

This decentralised 'consensus' of whether the transactions are correct is what removes the need for the middle man and the ledger – i.e. the bank.

---

[29] 'Hash Cash' by Adam Back is one example of a previous attempt at a Digital Currency.

The reward for this is given in order to incentivise people to continue to support the network and verify the transactions and add them to the network.

Reward

The miners perform a hash function to attempt to be the lucky miner that gets to add a particular block to the network. This is the last piece of data required in the block before the block can be added to the network. This 'effort' exerted by the computers in performing the hash function is the 'Proof of Work' element. They are solving a mathematical puzzle – a guess of a number actually – by using a hashing algorithm known as SHA-256 which basically searches for a random number and tries each and every number until the Bitcoin software acknowledges that the number is correct. The block then gets added to the blockchain. The reward in BTC is given to the miner who found the number.

The process then starts again with the new block of transactions. This happens roughly every 10 minutes.

The computational effort required was built in because there needs to be some work required to earn this currency (BTC) in order to give it some value. If there was no effort spent there would be no value to the output – i.e. BTC[30]

Immutability

In the Bitcoin blockchain, each block of data or transaction data is connected to the previous one and this creates the chain of blocks. The sequence of these blocks cannot be changed because certain data points in each block point to the previous block. Firstly there is a timestamp. More specifically the 'hash' of the previous block is always included in the new block.

---

[30] This is quite an old economic concept and applies to gold and other hard to get items. The effort to produce something gives it value.

The 'hash' of a block is like the unique abbreviation of all of the data in that block to create a condensed reference for that block. A postcode is a simple hash for all of the houses in a given area. This is important because if anyone tried to change any of the data in a particular block retrospectively, then the hash output (the postcode for example) would be different and therefore the next block would not link back to it correctly. And this would be spotted on the network.

If you see Fig 1. below you will see that the previous block hash is actually combined with the data from the current block thus forming its own new block hash. This block hash is then used by the following block for the same purpose. It can be tricky to get your head around but essentially data is hashed together and linked from block to block.

In this way the blockchain offers this continuous and immutable quality for such a network that Bitcoin was created to be.

Figure 1. Diagram of data from a Bitcoin Block. See transaction data (Tx100 etc.) and block hashes. There is more data on top of this but this illustrates what I am trying to demonstrate.[31]

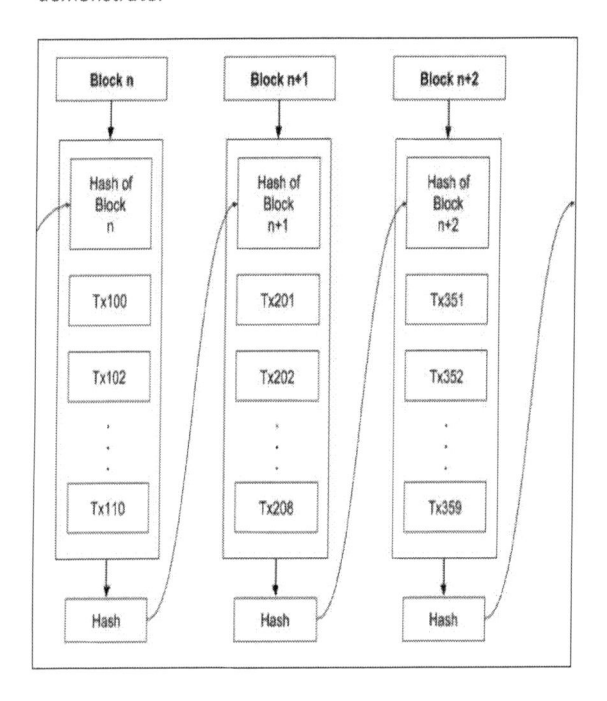

I will add at this point that on YouTube there is a free 26 lecture MIT course on Blockchain/Cryptocurrency taught by Gary Gensler from 2017/18. This is an excellent course and one I have listened to and learned from. Each lecture is 1 hour 15 mins. Browse the topics for each lecture and choose which you want to listen to. It covers the above in great detail and much more. The example of a postcode as a hash function is one I borrowed from him![32]

---

[31] Source: www.tutorialspoint.com/blockchain/blockchain_chaining_blocks.htm
[32] MIT Open Courseware, Prof. Gary Gensler (2018)
https://ocw.mit.edu/courses/15-s12-blockchain-and-money-fall-2018/resources/session-1-introduction/

Ironically Gary Gensler is not very popular now in the crypto world as he is head of the US Securities and Exchange Commission (SEC) and is causing regulatory problems for crypto exchanges!

I will also add that the Bitcoin Whitepaper by Satoshi Nakamoto is worth reading as well. It's quite short. Certain parts are hard to understand from a technical point of view but the essence can be more than sufficiently understood by the average individual.[33]

The Benefit of Bitcoin and the Reason it was Created

So in conclusion as you can see in the example of Bitcoin:

The need for it to exist is the belief that there is a benefit to creating a Digital Currency on a Blockchain – the aim was to create a Decentralised peer to peer payment network with a currency that could not be double spent! The Reward was required to incentivise the people who 'mine' to keep all of the transactions accurate so there are no errors and the system is trustworthy.

The reason I am stressing this in bold is that to those who believe that the banking system needs to be improved, Bitcoin is solving a problem and this is *why* it exists. Blockchain technology, the hash function and its rewards mechanism facilitates this.[34]

Satoshi Nakamoto inserted this message in the genesis block of Bitcoin:

---

[33] https://bitcoin.org/bitcoin.pdf?
[34] All of the technology, mechanisms and ideas used in Bitcoin existed previously. What Satoshi Nakamoto did was to combine different elements and mechanisms together to create Bitcoin.

"The Times 03/Jan/2009 Chancellor on brink of second bailout for banks"

So this suggests that Satoshi Nakamoto, whoever he/she/they are or were, saw the current banking system as a problem and this (i.e. Bitcoin) is a proposed solution.

Assessing Cryptocurrencies as an Investment

So the first question to ask when assessing a cryptocurrency is – Why does it exist? What problem is it solving? Is this valuable and will it still be valuable (or more valuable) in the future.

The truth is that for many existing cryptocurrencies it is hard to justify why they exist.

The use-case for a cryptocurrency is often referred to in the crypto space as the 'Utility' of a currency.

There are approx. 16000 cryptocurrencies in existence right now. The vast majority of them are not useful nor required to solve a problem. Some are out and out scams just to get money from people. Some are potentially very useful.

This is why the first question when trying to assess a cryptocurrency has to be – what is it doing? Why does it exist? Is it useful and will it be useful at some point in the future?

Tokenomics

Another important factor to consider when understanding and assessing cryptocurrencies as an investment is their 'tokenomics'.

This is their 'token-economics' if you like, which takes into consideration:

How many tokens/coins are in circulation?

What is the maximum supply of the coin/token in the future?

What is the annual inflation rate?

What is the vesting schedule / unlock rate?

Market Cap of the token/coin?

How distributed is the token/coin supply?

How liquid is the token / coin?

These factors are important because you can gain an understanding of potential value of the cryptocurrency based on the various factors. For example if the annual inflation rate of a currency is high then the currency becomes devalued over time as new coins come onto the market. Whereas a cryptocurrency with low inflation may be a better investment.

Similarly with regard the token distribution of a currency, if you can see that 40% of the total supply of a currency is held by 2 or 3 individuals/wallets, then you need to consider that if these people decide to sell their 40% share of the currency, then the price will go down as they release them for sale on the market.

Finally regarding the liquidity of a coin, it is good to know that there is a large daily trading volume of an asset because it means there is demand for the currency. So if and when you do want to sell your investment, there will be buyers around to buy it from you. If you hold a very small and obscure cryptocurrency that has low daily trading volume (liquidity) then when you choose to sell any then you may struggle to do so.

I am going to use the 2 cryptocurrencies Bitcoin (BTC) and Optimism (OP) as examples. These are sufficiently different to show examples of contrasting tokenomics.

Bitcoin (BTC)

Circulating supply: 19,274,500 BTC (91.8% of total supply)

Maximum supply: 21,000,000 BTC

Issuance and Inflation – 1.83% per annum

Market Cap – $443,732,000,000 – the value of each coin $23,021 multiplied by total coins in circulation 19,274,500

Coin Allocation / Distribution – Fair launch. i.e. anyone could mine this from day 1. No-one was awarded any at the outset.

Liquidity (daily trading volume) - $24,500,000,000

No of wallets – 44 million approx

Daily Active users – 640,000

So Bitcoin has 92% of it's supply already in circulation. It's inflation rate is currently 1.83% per annum (this will halve in 2024 to become less than 1% inflation).

It has a high market cap of $443 billion and a daily trading volume of $24.5 billion. This is excellent liquidity.

It's distribution is good with no one entity obviously owning more than 1% of the whole supply.[35]

---

[35] Satoshi Nakamoto is believed to have mined over 1 million BTC in the early days. What are believed to be his wallet(s) are visible and have remained

Optimism (OP)[36]

Circulating supply: 314,000,000 (7% of total supply)

Maximum supply: 4,290,000,000

Issuance and Inflation –per annum – see vesting schedule below

Vesting schedule / Unlock rate: 3.8 billion over 3.5 years = average of 2.97 million tokens per day

Market Cap – $765,000,000 – the value of each coin $2.44 multiplied by total coins in circulation 314,000,000

Distribution: 17% Investors, 19% Core Contributors, 19% User Airdrops, 25% Ecosystem Fund, 20% Retroactive Goods Funding

Liquidity (daily trading volume) - $290,000,000

Daily active users – 60,000

Total Value Locked - $925 million

---

untouched since his exit from the scene. This is the exception where someone owns a significant amount.

[36] Data for BTC and OP is collated March/April 2023 from: Coin Market Cap (https://coinmarketcap.com/currencies/bitcoin/ and https://coinmarketcap.com/currencies/optimism/), Token Unlocks (https://token.unlocks.app/optimism) , Token Terminal (https://tokenterminal.com/terminal/projects/bitcoin and https://tokenterminal.com/terminal/projects /optimism) DeFi Lama (https://defilama.com/chain/optimism?tvl=true) These are all useful analytics platforms to indicate activity on blockchains as well as usage volume and data

Optimism has only 7% of its total supply in circulation.

With 3.8 billion of tokens unlocking (see vesting schedule above) in the next 3.5 years until August 2026, that's 25% per year of new tokens on the market.

This token unlock / inflation rate increases the supply enormously over the next three and a half years.

This is potentially very high selling pressure over the next few years and so the price of Optimism could easily be held back by this selling pressure.[37]

The market cap is below $1 billion so is relatively low. The liquidity however is excellent relative to its market cap and so for now this token is very liquid.

The token distribution for Optimism has 17% allocated to early investors and 19% allocated to 'Core Contributors' – this will be the development and management team I would expect. So you have 36% of tokens being held by what will be a relatively small number of people. I have seen worse distributions than this. However there are potentially a lot of tokens there in few hands. This means that should any of these individuals decide to sell at any time, this could have an impact on the price.

As you can see these 2 investments present 2 very different propositions. The tokenomics are very different and so the investor has a lot to consider. The long term investor would prefer the low inflation rate of Bitcoin and the fact that over 90% of the total supply is already on the market.

---

[37] I would add that after August 2026 there should be no more tokens to unlock as the max supply should have been reached. This will change the equation dramatically assuming the tokenomics have not changed in that time.

Optimism in contrast has a potentially high sell pressure from the vesting schedule and the inflation rate. The fact that only 7% of coins are now in circulation is actually quite scary.

However the low market cap and very high relative trading volume for Optimism mean that the price will be very volatile. The price could swing upwards very quickly making an excellent short term investment. However this could also happen in the other direction – the price could go down very quickly.

Optimism presently sits at around $2.44 per coin. It is gaining users everyday. It is a Layer 2 scaling solution for Ethereum and so this potentially is a great use-case. So an investor may decide that the utility and the trend for Layer 2s to grow at this current time will make Optimism a good near term investment, with a view to adjusting the thesis as time evolves.

So all of these factors of the tokenomics give you an understanding of the asset and it's potential behaviour. They do not determine whether it is a good investment or not but they do significantly contribute to the overall picture for decision making.

Market Capitalisation (Market Cap)

The price of a cryptocurrency, or a stock for that matter, is not necessarily as important as the Market Cap.

Take Cardano (ADA) for example, it's price is around 0.38 cents, there are 34.8 billion ADA in circulating supply and has a market cap of $13.4 billion.

Now take Solana (SOL), it's price is $21.85, there are 393 million in circulating supply and the market cap is $8.5 billion

So the price of a Solana (SOL) token is 57 times more than the price of a Cardano token (ADA).

The Market Cap of Solana is less than Cardano.

As you can see the market cap is more important to understand to assess the value of a cryptocurrency because the price is dependant on the amount of tokens in circulation. The Market Cap is the collective valuation of all of the coins together and so it is relevant to compare Market Caps more than actual dollar prices of cryptos when deciding which cryptos to invest in. A smaller Market Cap has higher risk, yet often higher upside potential because the price can be moved with less buy pressure than a coin with a higher market cap.

Solana and Cardano have quite similar market caps. If you compare one of them to Bitcoin which has a market cap of $443 billion, you can see the difference. It will take a lot more buy pressure to move BTC by 10% than it would to move SOL or ADA by 10%.[38]

Bitcoin – and my Relationship with it!

I have covered earlier in Part 3 what Bitcoin is and why it came about. It has taken me quite some time and studying to really come to understand what it is and how it works. There are a lot of parts to the technology and the mechanisms involved.

---

[38] Data from Coin Market Cap, April 2023 -
https://coinmarketcap.com/currencies/solana/ and
https://coinmarketcap.com/currencies/cardano/

I recommended the MIT course on YouTube by Gary Gensler previously. This course goes into great detail about what Bitcoin is and how it's mechanisms work.

As I've continued to study Bitcoin, new elements continue to sink in and pennies continue drop about the significance of certain things.

I remain curious and will continue to study and absorb information about it. I remain an investor only really. There are people termed 'Bitcoin Maxis' who completely buy into Bitcoin's ethos and believe it is the future and they are steadfast in their opinions and determination to help to grow the network.

Often Bitcoin Maxis reject all other cryptocurrencies as inferior and not worthy of investment. This is not where I sit. I am an investor and see potential value in Bitcoin as well as other cryptocurrencies. Nevertheless I see Bitcoin as the safest potential investment in the crypto space.

I have mentioned some of the design features of Bitcoin already. For example how it is mined. There is also programmed in a mechanism that adjusts the mining difficulty to keep a frequent reward for the miners. Another feature is the hard capped supply. This maximum supply of 21 million Bitcoins is it's answer to the current global 'monetary policy' of printing more fiat currency[39] and devaluing it.

People see BTC as 'Sound Money' as well as the decentralised peer to peer payment system that it was designed to be.

My relationship with Bitcoin as an investor is an interesting one.

So as per the introduction to this book I first bought a small amount of Bitcoin on an exchange called Ziglu back in 2020. Almost instantly Bitcoin was losing value and I could not handle this volatility. I sold out pretty quickly and

---

[39] Fiat currency is currency that is not backed by anything except the word of the central bank or government that provides the money. This covers the majority of global currencies right now. Fiat can be printed at will and therefore ultimately devalued

even though it was a small amount of funds, my first experience was not a good one.

I guess now I was just probably buying a top and wasn't ready for the volatility.

Again as I mentioned when I bought back into crypto properly with Coinbase in late 2021, I didn't rush to buy Bitcoin. I guess I saw altcoins (i.e. all cryptocurrencies except Bitcoin) as more volatile and therefore potentially more rewarding. Also Bitcoin was again beginning a downtrend from November 2021. Bitcoin also generally 'leads' the crypto market. If the Bitcoin price is increasing, then generally most other cryptocurrencies will be going up in it's wake. The same is true if Bitcoin is decreasing in price; if the price is decreasing then the majority of other cryptocurrencies will also be decreasing in price, but at a faster rate.

So again having held a lot of other cryptocurrencies from the beginning, Bitcoin was seemingly leading the downtrend and not helping my investments, or 'bets.' So this was another negative association with Bitcoin at this point.

Ironically though, as I live through this current bear market with prices having tumbled down, I have learned about Bitcoin and have flipped a lot of my initial altcoin investments into Bitcoin. I have also bought a lot more Bitcoin along the way as well, especially around the low prices below $20,000.

So, strangely, despite this downward trend and seemingly negative experience. Bitcoin has grown on me. I have studied it and understand why it should be a significant part of my crypto portfolio. What I have learned about the technology is impressive and it seems to me like it could be a worthwhile investment. This is all despite not having made any profits at all in this thing! I feel like it's really testing me!

Bitcoin Market Cycles

One of the things I have learned about Bitcoin is the impact the Bitcoin 'Halving' has had on the price since its inception.

Bitcoin's market cycles revolve around this famous 'Halving' as well as some well known emotional investing states that we humans are prone to repeating.

I have previously mentioned that the Flux cryptocurrency has its own halving. I fully expect that it got this inspiration from Bitcoin.

The Bitcoin Halving is the reduction by half of the Block Reward for the Bitcoin miners on the network. So each Block is produced or 'mined' every 10 minutes on average. When this block is added to the Bitcoin blockchain this generates a reward in Bitcoin to the miner. This is known as the 'Block Reward'.

Initially in 2009 the Block Reward was programmed to be 50 Bitcoins for every block. This would be then be halved every 210,000 blocks – which is roughly every 4 years, with a block added every 10 minutes. It's worth mentioning here that the Bitcoin mining 'difficulty' is automatically adjusted every 2 weeks to maintain this approximate 10 minute block reward. This is how it can maintain a consistent reward for the miners. This has been programmed in because the creator(s) realised that rewarding or incentivising the miners is a key part of Bitcoin's value and so this had to be programmed to maintain some consistency in the network.

So the Halving is cyclically reducing the amount of Bitcoin issued every 4 years. The initial block reward was 50 BTC, then 25 BTC, then 12.5 BTC, and we currently sit at 6.25 BTC.

Why is this important?

First of all the issuance of new Bitcoin is essentially Bitcoin's inflation rate. So at present the BTC inflation rate is 1.83%.

When the Block reward halves in approx. March 2024 the inflation rate will be around 0.9% per annum. Of course this roughly halves again in approx. 2028 and so on.

So compared with other currencies this current inflation rate is extremely good. And of course it will get even better with time. Inflation typically devalues a currency. Currencies such as the US Dollar and GB Pound Sterling 'aim' for an annual inflation rate of 2%. This target is frequently missed to the upside and for example we have just seen inflation upwards of 10% in the last year.

As time goes on decreasing amounts of BTC being produced and more fiat currency being printed should give rise to price appreciation for BTC (and other assets) when compared to fiat currencies.

The second implication of the Halving to mention is the impact on mining economics:

Miners have a cost of running their 'miners' (computers on the network). They will have an electricity/power cost and also hardware costs to cover. Therefore a portion of mining or 'block rewards' will be used, i.e. SOLD, to cover these costs. The remainder will be the miner's profit – i.e. the incentive for running and securing the Bitcoin network.

So miners will sell BTC to cover costs and will either keep the profits in BTC, or convert it to USD for example. In theory then there is currently, as of March 2023, potentially 6.25 BTC being sold every 10 minutes by the miners. For the Bitcoin price to remain the same then there will be an equal amount of buyers.

So when the block reward is halved, the amount of BTC being sold every 10 minutes has halved, simply because there is less in issuance to the miners. So if in March 2024 the block reward is 3.125 BTC, then there can only be 3.125 new BTC sold by the miners every 10 minutes. IF (and it's a big if!!) the buying demand for BTC remains constant at 6.25 BTC which, for this example, WAS holding the price steady when block reward was 6.25 BTC, then there is now more Buyers than Sellers, thus increasing the price of BTC.

The economics are a little more complicated than this of course. The miner profit and expenses are totally dependant on the price of BTC at the time of mining. As we know this fluctuates. A lot! But there are critical levels below which miners can't operate. Miners have BTC flowing constantly but have to make constant decisions about whether to just cover costs or whether to sell or 'HODL' their BTC profits. This will vary from miner to miner. However there are critical BTC price levels below which miners find it very difficult to cover costs. Therefore only the most efficient mining set ups will survive as the BTC price goes down. We have recently seen this with miners such as Argo Blockchain having hit financial difficulty. When the BTC price was around $60,000, miners had to decide whether to sell for instant profits or hold in case the price keeps going up.

I digress slightly, but the point is that mining economics are a crucial part of the BTC network and it's value. The other major part affecting demand is of course investor speculation and genuine demand for BTC. By genuine demand for BTC, I mean people who are actually using BTC for payments.

In summary then, the reduction in BTC rewards effectively reduces the amount of new BTC available to sell on the open market and therefore create downward pressure on the price. On it's own, in theory this is positive for the price. However if we look at the following chart to see what has happened historically, we can see how the 4 year 'Halving cycle' has thus far affected the BTC price.

Figure 2. Bitcoin Market Cycles Chart. y axis is Price. x axis is date[40]

FIGURE 2: **BITCOIN MARKET CYCLES: PRICE VS. REALIZED PRICE**[3]

Ignore the thin line and see the darker thicker line (the jagged line) which is the historic Bitcoin Price. (This was the best chart I could find to show what I wanted without creating my own!)

---

[40] Chart taken from IBKRCampus Traders' Insight (19 July 2022) 'Crypto Market Cycles.' (Original source for chart – 'Grayscale' grayscale.com) ibkrcampus.com/traders-insight/securities/crypto/crypto-market-cycles/

You can explain the previous chart by breaking each cycle into 4 parts:

Table 1. Data is taken from Digital Asset News[41] YouTube channel. Edited slightly.

	Cycle 1	BTC price	Cycle 2	BTC price	Cycle 3	BTC price
Block Reward	25 BTC		12.5 BTC		6.25 BTC	
Halving Year	2012	$10	2016	$375-$956	2020	$4,900-$29,000
All Time High	2013	$1,132	2017	$19,500	2021	$67,617
Correction	2014	$314	2018	$3,232	2022	$15,742
Reset	2015	$200 - $460	2019	$3,400-$12,900	2023	?

So as you can see the Halving has had a similar effect for the first 3 Halvings. The price has shot up within 12-18 months of the Halving each time. This will be partially due to BTC mining economics, partly due to macro economics facilitating speculation and also the fact that Bitcoin is maturing and gaining users.

This final reason is of course vital. Bitcoin has only been around for 14 years and so is very young still. From a standing start it has had exponential growth which one can't expect to continue at the same rate. As I have said before, an asset with a small market cap can be moved easily, however an asset with

---

[41] youtube.com/@DigitalAssetNews

a higher market cap (i.e. Bitcoin as it grows) takes significantly more inflows of capital to move a similar amount in percentage terms.

As for what's in store over the next couple of years, who knows? If the cycle plays out in a similar way the BTC price will appreciate. Is this one of the best 'bets' you will ever see? Time will tell. There are 2 significant factors looming that will impact Bitcoin and it's price. They are macro economics as well as United States and worldwide crypto regulation.

The macro economics are important because they will determine the liquidity in the system. To me, this factor could be lining up perfectly. We have had very high inflation leading to an extreme tightening of liquidity in the US and across the globe. Signs right now are that this tightening could abate in 2023 and perhaps ease into 'loosening' and interest rate decreases across 2024 and 2025. This could really support BTC over 2024 and 2025 in its 'Halving' and subsequent potential 'All Time High' years. In fact this seems almost too good to be true. We will see.

Crypto regulation is looming, and actually happening as we speak. This could impact the BTC price either negatively or positively depending on which governments or institutions decide to regulate and to what extent. Will it be positive for crypto? Or will it try to supress it? Will only BTC be allowed to flourish, or will it also be quashed? Who knows. We will see. Crypto has a lot going for it as a technology but has a lot of problems as well.

Macro Economics

I have had to learn an awful lot about macro economics as a crypto investor. Up to now my previous share investments have been buy, hold and forget shares or some sort of Index fund via a bank. Therefore I've never really studied the impact of global liquidity on the value or price of any shares I was holding. Yes I would notice that a fund was down in an economic downturn but I understood that these swings are part of the market and that they would ultimately swing back up again.

As I have entered the crypto investing world I have tried to learn a lot about the technology and therefore how and where to invest. In doing this I have found a crypto-wide obsession with the price of Bitcoin and what is happening with the price all the time. Everyday. I've just sort of fallen in to this and I wasn't really expecting this and where it would lead in terms of macro economic understanding.

It seems Bitcoin is very correlated to stocks and share indices, particularly the Nasdaq and S&P 500. I have also heard it referred to as an 'index of global liquidity.'[42] This essentially means that the price of Bitcoin is also correlated to the amount of liquidity in the system, which is largely dependant on Central Bank interest rates and the availability of capital.

I have also come across an obsession of 'Money Printing' commentary. This 'money printing' is officially known as 'Quantitative Easing' and is where a government will create money by borrowing from it's central bank. I.e. the Central Bank issues new debt that a government can pay back in the future (in theory). It is basically a way of creating more money – hence the term 'money printing.'

Of course this Quantitative Easing or Money Printing **is** global liquidity. If governments are creating new money and injecting it into an economy then this means they are trying to stimulate economic activity. Low interest rates also help to stimulate activity as well. Low interest rates make it inexpensive to borrow money, and at the same time not very rewarding to hold onto money in a savings account.

So when there are low interest rates and some stimulus in the form of Quantitative Easing, then liquidity in the system increases and this also finds its way to stocks and crypto asset investing, as well as generally increasing day to day high street activity. Therefore this liquidity is what can drive the price of assets such as Bitcoin in the short term. Ultimately the value of any

---

[42] youtube.com/moneyzg - YouTube channel Money ZG, James on here frequently refers to Bitcoin as an 'index of global liquidity'

asset, and in this case Bitcoin, has to be in it's fundamental value or utility rather than relying on cheap liquidity to fuel it's price.

The crypto community's obsession with money printing is precisely because Bitcoin is the antithesis of this. Bitcoin has a hard capped supply of 21 million Bitcoins. The last one is forecast to be created around 2140. There will never be any more. As I have mentioned the Bitcoin inflation rate is approx. 1.8% today. This will roughly half to 0.9% in 2024. Then in 2028 it will roughly half again to 0.4% ish. Et Cetera.

Contrast this with the US Dollar in the US, whose inflation rate target is 2% and this is quite often 'missed' and leads to inflation above these levels which can be 10% or more. Global currencies are based on the FIAT system. Whereby they are not backed by any collateral. Any central bank can just issue new debt to a government and hey presto you have effectively created more of that currency from thin air. So the printing of new money devalues or 'debases' a currency by putting more in circulation.

Previously the US Dollar was on the 'Gold standard' and the US government/central bank was in theory obliged to hold the equivalent value of gold in reserve for every dollar in circulation. So if it needed any more dollars then gold had to be the collateral to be able to get it. However this was abolished in the 1970s by Richard Nixon. This opened the door to what we now see as creating new money by asking central banks to issue new government debt when required.

Figure 3. Chart from Statista.com Original source is US department of the Treasury. May 2023[43]

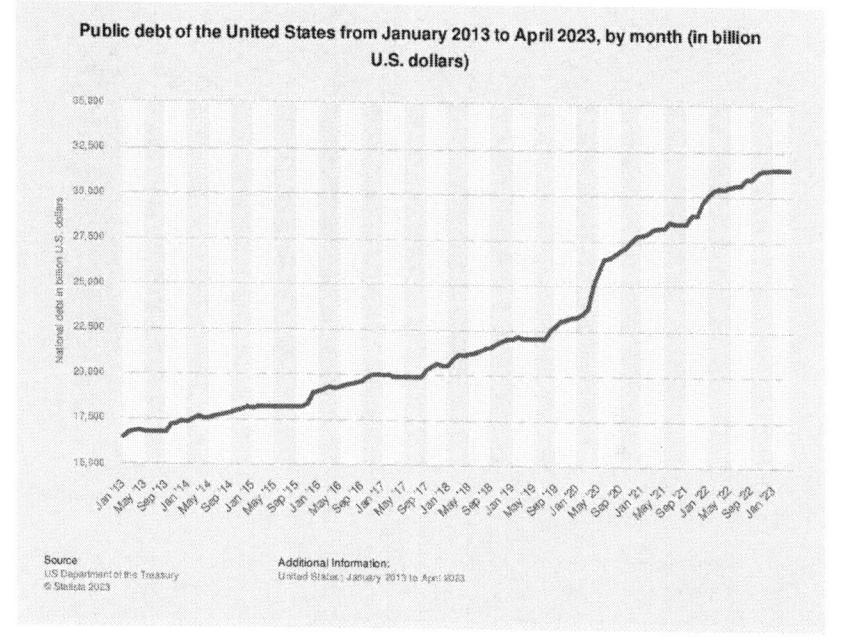

Public debt of the United States from January 2013 to April 2023, by month (in billion U.S. dollars)

As a result of lots of new debt issuance from the 'Quantitative Easing', government debts around the globe have risen a lot. Over the Covid pandemic the US has increased the number of dollars in circulation significantly. You can see the spike in Figure 3. So that is the extra debt that was taken on during the pandemic.

---

[43] From Statista.com Original data source: US Treasury (May 2023) https://www.statista.com/statistics/273294/public-debt-of-the-united-states-by-month/

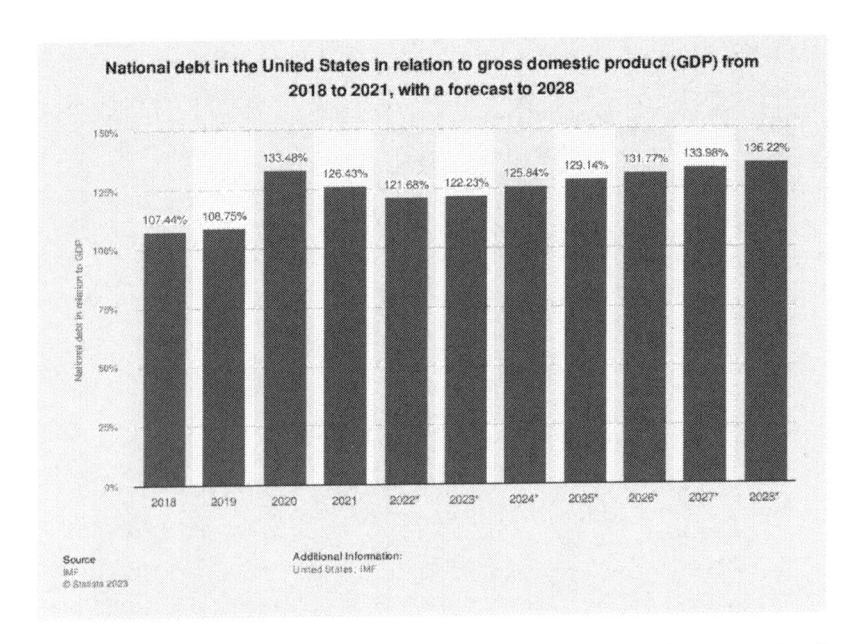

Figure 4. Chart from Statista.com Original source IMF (International Monetary Fund). Published by IMF April 2023[44]

The US debt to GDP ratio is around 130% now. One analyst who I subscribe to on his YouTube channel, 'Invest Answers' explains that this is beyond the point of retrieval.[45] He often explains that the US government debt is in an upward spiral. It can no longer be brought under control and paid back. There are similar stories around the globe, debt to GDP ratios are out of control and tax receipts and other income for governments are barely enough to service the debt costs, let alone pay down the debt.

---

[44] From Statista.com Original data source: International Monetary Fund (IMF) (April 2023) https://www.statista.com/statistics/269960/national-debt-in-the-us-in-relation-to-gross-domestic-product-gdp/#:~:text=The%20statistic%20shows%20the%20national,US%20GDP%20for%20further%20information.

[45] youtube.com/investanswers - Invest Answers is hosted by a chap called James who delves into data in great detail. I've learned an awful lot from this channel about macro economics as well as trading and investment strategies

The recent increase in interest rates is a double-edged sword for governments such as in the US. The US Federal Reserve has hiked interest rates at an unprecedented speed in 2022. This is aimed at controlling inflation by reducing demand within the economy. However the unfortunate by-product of this is that this interest rate also applies to the US government debt. The US government debt is very high and increasing the interest rates also increases the interest that the US government has to pay back to the Federal Reserve. So on the one hand the inflation rate may be coming down, however the debt servicing costs for the government are growing significantly.

Raising debt ceilings and printing more money is the only way to service this debt.[46]

Similarly on a more individual level, personal borrowing is very high in particularly in western society now. Many people have mortgages and other borrowings. Interest rates around the world have been so low for so long since the 2008 financial crisis that people have just taken on debt at an unprecedented level. To have interest rates spike so quickly in 2022 has hurt the individual borrower as well. Anyone re-mortgaging their home in late 2022 or now in 2023 will see a huge increase in borrowing costs. So much that potentially the cost is unsustainable.

When a debt becomes unsustainable for an individual then an asset such as a home may well have to be sold or worse, forcibly repossessed. This can be catastrophic on a personal level.

For a government they can perform 'Quantitative Easing' or print some more money to service the debt but this in turn will eventually devalue the currency.

---

[46] The US is about to vote to raise it's debt ceiling again in June 2023

This paints a gloomy picture of global debt and future inflation rates. It's quite doom and gloom really. Personally I still study and learn about this and so I'm sure I'll uncover more as time goes on.

However I will note that as I have learned this it did flag a penny dropping moment that I once had in the past when looking at share prices. Having studied some shares occasionally and held a few, mainly since 2020, I did look into some price charts of certain shares and basically saw a continuous upward trend over time in most assets. One night the penny dropped that it is basically increasing as the currency devalues over time. So in the same way a can of Coca-Cola was 35p back in the day, it is now at least £1. So in the last 15 years or so the price of a can of Coca-Cola has perhaps tripled. When in actual fact the currency, GBP, has in fact devalued as it's buying power is now less.

This seems rudimentary now but it's of course probably the most pivotal part to understanding why to invest in assets and not hold cash. The old fashioned mantra to save all of your money in cash (or savings accounts) I'm afraid has probably not been the best idea in the last 20 years or so.

So essentially asset prices continue to go up as global currencies debase themselves due to inflation and quantitative easing. The value of assets (i.e. their prices) are going up against the US dollar or against the GB pound for example. More currency chasing the same assets will drive asset prices up if the volume of assets do not increase at the same rate as the volume of currency in circulation.

People theorise that for Bitcoin, if it is allowed to flourish, the prices of everyday items should go up at a far less significant rate versus the Bitcoin price, if indeed they increase at all. Bitcoin's inflation rate is decreasing every 4 years. So while Bitcoin is slightly inflationary, and indeed getting less so, it is far less inflationary than other currencies. Therefore the Bitcoin price versus other currencies will likely go up due to this. It is fairly basic economics, however it does of course depend on the adoption or even simply the general acceptance of Bitcoin. This explains why many see Bitcoin as a store of value or 'Digital Gold.'

Bitcioin is a 'Hard Asset' with a fixed supply and a decreasing inflation rate. This is the opposite of FIAT currencies.[47]

Another macro economic factor that may affect the trajectory of asset prices is political stability or rather political instability. The Russia Ukraine conflict of 2022 created a downward pressure on asset prices due to general instability and economic concern around the region and around the globe. There can also be direct impact as there has been on commodities in this case. The energy supply has been significantly affected due to this conflict. This has pushed energy prices up significantly in Europe. This directly affects liquidity in Europe. People and business need energy and therefore simply have to pay the higher prices. This means less money elsewhere including for speculative investments in assets whether it is housing, stocks or crypto assets.

Similarly tensions between other countries can create market uncertainty and affect asset prices. Markets, that is stock markets, commodity markets etc., are always trying to look forward and see what will be the situation in 3-6 months or 18-24 months time. This is so that investors can make their investments in the hope of taking their profits in that time frame. Political factors can affect this and hence markets react to any potential global tensions or conflict.

Technical Analysis of Price Charts

Price Charts is not something I was expecting to become especially familiar with at all. Cryptocurrencies are also known as 'Digital Assets' and are pretty

---

[47] This in part could explain the fear of worldwide authorities towards Bitcoin. The IMF has just approved a debt deal with Argentina on the proviso that it discourages crypto usage. Engler, A (18th March 2023) Coin Desk https://www.coindesk.com/policy/2022/03/18/argentine-congress-approves-imf-debt-deal-that-would-discourage-crypto-usage/

well their own asset class. Examples of other asset classes that investors trade are Stocks, Traditional Currencies, Government Bonds, Commodities such as oil or wheat, Property (Real Estate in US) and Precious Metals.

So Digital Assets sit alongside these as an asset class that investors trade to earn money from. Of course this involves moving in and out of these assets – aka buying and selling – in order to make a profit.

Price charts for stocks and cryptocurrencies are obviously the current and historical trading price for that asset.

Below are a list of things that may affect the price of a traditional stock like McDonalds for example:

Earnings reports – usually quarterly reports

Forecast earnings reports

Growth plans

Current and future competition in that niche

Current leadership credentials and potential

These factors combined can determine people's decision whether to invest in a stock or not.

For cryptocurrency this is a bit different because there are not always profit and loss reports in the same way there are for stocks.

However there are factors that can help to gauge how well a cryptocurrency project is growing and how it is doing versus it's competition. These are metrics such as:

Total Value locked in a DeFi protocol

Daily Active Users

Number of transactions in a given period

Fees earned in a given period – say by Uniswap DEX for example

Road Map for growth – Usually in a 'White Paper' individual to each Cryptocurrency project

So as you can see there are similarities but the data is not submitted in the same way that traditional stocks have to report their figures as publicly owned companies.

While there are fundamental aspects to trying to value a cryptocurrency or more particularly a stock, over years and years price charts have been studied and it has become clear that these price charts are fundamentally a representation of the human emotions of traders and investors.

There are many different indicators that can be used to assess price charts. Some basic features include:

Support and Resistance levels

Trendlines

Heikin-Ashi Candles

Moving averages

To expand on a basic one which is **Support and Resistance levels**, this is simply a price where there may be a lot of support for an asset.

So for example Bitcoin has a lot of support around $25,000 level.

Therefore traders will have read the historic charts and know that many buyers will come in when the price dips down to $25,000.

So if BTC is trading at $27,000 in an upward trending market, then $25,000 may be a good place to set an automatic Buy order because if the price does drop, then it is likely to immediately bounce up off this level thus putting the trader into a profitable position.

However in a down trending market these levels can flip and become **Resistance** instead of Support.

So if BTC is trading at $23,000 then a trader may place an automatic Sell order at $25,000 because this area is possibly where other traders will aim to sell their BTC. This is because historically this has been an area of high volume where people may sell in a downward trend.

The trader may then wish to buy back the BTC at the lower price of $23,000 thus making a profit.

So in some ways these price charts can be a bit self-fulfilling in theory. Hence traders can trade by them so that the percentage chances of making a profit are in their favour. Of course it is not as simple as trading support and resistance levels *all* of the time – that would be too easy! But when you combine a number of factors, including the global economic or political outlook, as well as some more technical factors as I have listed above, then traders can place trades that have a high probability of making a profit.

If a trader makes many equal value trades then they just need to be right more that they are wrong as well as taking appropriate losses or profits at the correct times. Sounds easy!

I have become familiar with the basics of these charts and how to read them, however I am not a trader and do not have the time to study all the details to attempt to be a short term trader really. I do have a grasp of it and of particular interest to me has been the psychology of it all. As I explained the charts basically reflect human investor psychology. Benjamin Cowen has a website and YouTube channel called 'Into The Cryptoverse.'[48] On the channel he is often comparing current price charts with historical price charts from similar economic periods. The similarities are very obvious to see. This does not mean that the same thing plays out every time, however the trends can often be mapped very clearly to a previous period in time where economic conditions were similar.

The **Heikin-Ashi Candles** chart also got my attention when I came across it. Heikin-Ashi was a Japanese chap who closely studied the markets and produced a formula in order to better represent a price chart to show whether an asset is in an overall up-trend or down-trend. The patterns that emerge from these charts have historically been good indicators of which assets may be good to hold onto or not.

There are many such indicators like the Heikin-Ashi candles that traders use. Typically traders will make decisions based on a confluence of several indicators. For example if the Support lines, Heikin-Ashi chart and also some macro factors are all telling the same story, this is 3 ticks towards deciding whether to take a particular trade or not. A trader may use 10 indicators, 7 of which may be flashing BUY and the other 3 may be flashing neutral or SELL. So the trader may then make the call that the odds are in their favour to place the trade.

Holding Crypto for Yield is Dangerous!

As outlined in Part 2 of this book, I have had experiences where I have played with crypto to access the yields on offer. This included liquidity providing

---

[48] https://www.youtube.com/@intothecryptoverse and https://intothecryptoverse.com/

with Fantom, investing in Yield Nodes and also playing with some other 'Degen DeFi' projects.

The above examples didn't end well. The yields on offer were high and therefore risky. However the general downward trend of the crypto market and other asset classes was a significant factor in their lack of success.

I think the take away lesson is just that high yields are a reward for taking risk. They are there to entice people in. They can be a complete scam, or just an ill thought out project which is unsustainable. But also as I did mention, agile yield farmers can get in and out of these projects and make some serious money. This requires a vast understanding of what is going on and any contributing factors. It also requires time and some experience.

Having stated that some yields represent risk, I have mentioned that a key concept within crypto is that cryptocurrency is the reward for contributing to a decentralised network. Whether that is securing a network as a validator or miner, or offering the computational power such as storage to a network. The cryptocurrency is a reward that incentivises this network contribution. This is a very important concept and one that must be distinguished from high yield financial products within the DeFi space.

Nodes, miners and validators are necessary in a decentralised blockchain network and their incentivisation is important. Whether they are a worthwhile investment depends on the tokenomics of the project and also the use-case of what is trying to be achieved. Of course the use-case is a judgement that an investor or speculator will have to make on their own based on research.

In conclusion I'd say that understanding a project, where the incentive is coming from and what the incentive/reward means for the inflation/future value of the currency are key factors to be aware of before participating or investing.

"The Rules"

It's All Gone.

100% Scams

0% Exchanges

0% Leverage

Take Profits

Above are a funny yet poignant set of rules that are permanently on screen on the YouTube channel 'Digital Asset News.'[49]

I'll de-code them briefly. The overarching suggestion is that crypto is risky. It is the Wild West. Do not be surprised if you lose all of your investment. You need to be comfortable with this possibility. These rules will help keep both your funds safer and your expectations of the crypto space realistic!

It's all Gone – whatever amount you invest assume it's gone. Do not invest in crypto anything you can't live without. There's a chance you'll never see it again.

100% scams – Assume everything is a scam until proven otherwise.

0% Exchanges – If you invest in cryptocurrencies. Do not keep them on an exchange. Buy a 'Hardware wallet' – e.g. a Trezor wallet - and store your crypto on there. Keep nothing on Exchanges. If you leave crypto on an exchange you do not know what they are doing with it. Think FTX. Think Celsius etc. It may not be there when you want to sell or withdraw it.

---

[49] youtube.com/@DigitalAssetNews

0% leverage – do not use leverage. This is essentially borrowing money from an Exchange to trade with. Crypto prices are so volatile that this is very dangerous. If the market goes against you you will lose all of your money. Crypto is so volatile and unpredictable and you can trade on 10x or 100x leverage if you want to. Crypto is volatile enough without leverage.
If you use leverage one day you will get caught out even if you do well initially.

Take Profits – This is Rob's way of saying that if you get into a profit with an investment, take some profit off the table. Do not be greedy and expect your investment to multiply by 10 or 50 before taking any profit. Crypto is volatile and can turn quickly and profits you have been sat on (but not realised) can be wiped out very quickly. Have your profit targets *before* you enter a trade / investment and *stick to them*!

And they're the rules. Not a bad guide in my view!

Part 4: The State of Crypto in 2023

In this part I will discuss the current state of the cryptocurrency market as well as any factors that may affect the trajectory of cryptocurrencies and the blockchain technology that underpins them.

2022 was an horrific year for cryptocurrency.

Firstly the values of all cryptocurrencies have fallen dramatically from their all time high prices set in 2021.

Secondly the blow ups of Terra Luna, Celsius, Block-Fi, Voyager and FTX have been a HUGE black eye for the industry.

Crypto has already been plagued with 'Pump and Dump' schemes for years before now. There still exist many of these schemes as well.

'Pump and Dump' schemes are where people promote a coin or project and encourage new investors to buy into it, thus pushing up the price. The promoters will then sell when the price is where they want it to be. Thus they will take their profit and the coin will plummet in price, leaving the new investors with nothing of any value.

This all serves to give negative vibes for the industry. And this is absolutely fair. Crypto is an unregulated space where many people go in and come out with a huge black eye having been scammed or just not read the market properly. This leaves a bad impression and the news of this doesn't travel well.

There has always been the undercurrent of money laundering in crypto as well.

Mixers

As far as the issue of money laundering goes, crypto has within it's sphere technology known as 'Mixers.' One of these 'Mixers' is called Tornado Cash.

Tornado Cash is a protocol to where you can send cryptocurrency and it will 'mix' it with other people's cryptocurrency, create different wallet addresses for you and give the same amount of crypto back to you in a different wallet (or more than one different wallet).

So if you send in 2 ETH you would get 2 ETH back but not the very same 2 ETH that you sent into the mixer.

This is designed to obfuscate the trail of the funds and from where and whom they came.

The reason this is a 'thing' is because all cryptocurrency movements can been seen on the blockchain. If I send some ETH from one wallet to another then the whole of the transaction is completely publicly visible on Etherscan.io. Etherscan will show you the wallet address the funds were sent from and to. It will show you the amount, the time, the fee paid and which block it was in on the relevant blockchain – Ethereum in this example.

Some people do not want all of their transactions to be completely visible to all. Of course no one knows *who* owns what wallet from looking on Etherscan. The wallets are just a string of numbers and letters. However eventually these will lead back to a crypto Exchange such as Binance, which *does* hold your ID credentials and can therefore pin down who has done which transactions, or at least see who was involved in the trail of transactions.

There are other Exchanges though that *do not* hold your credentials and this can be a way of remaining anonymous. I do not use any exchanges that are completely anonymous and so cannot say I have experience of this. And regulations are tightening everywhere to avoid this practice of non-KYC exchanges (KYC is 'Know Your Customer').

So the long and the short of this is that people can attempt to launder money by trying to be anonymous and also 'mixing' the path or history of their crypto transaction by using these mixer services.

Ultimately all money has to come from somewhere so KYC exchange or non-KYC exchange, it's likely a bank was the original source and so hiding money on the blockchain is actually very difficult! So in reality it's one of the worst places for money laundering.

Nevertheless Mixers dilute crypto transaction history and create the problem of absolutely proving transaction history of some cryptocurrency.

As a result of this the US outlawed the use of Tornado Cash in 2022 and the developer who coded it is actually in jail awaiting trial for programming the protocol! A lot of the cryptocurrency community are understandably outraged by this. Their argument is that he has essentially coded some software that is not illegal. The use of it can be used effectively for illicit purposes but the developer has not in theory done anything wrong.

The theory behind the development of Tornado Cash in the first place is just to be able to keep some transactions private. They could be anonymous donations to charity or some other entity for example. An interesting debate this one I think!

An interesting point on this is that upon discussing cryptocurrency with an accountant, one of the only questions I recall him asking was about how people operate under the radar with crypto. I went onto to discuss this very fact about mixers with him.

This says a lot as it is the stand-out impression there is of the crypto market. A dangerous place with 'underworld' connotations. This was my original perception of crypto as well until I came into the space properly and began to educate myself and gained confidence in how it works, what it actually is and how to use cryptocurrency.

Privacy Coins

There are also cryptocurrencies called Privacy coins such as Monero (XMR). These also help to obscure the identity of the sender. When using Monero the transaction data is obscured so that you cannot see the exact amount of a transaction, nor can you see which wallet address sent or received the money. Contrast this to Ethereum and Bitcoin, where all the data is there for everyone to see.

So to move away from money laundering specifically, crypto is at a delicate point after such a terrible 2022.

I have listed some of the negative points so far but the truth is the technology is still exceptional. The transaction speed and cost is in many ways faster and cheaper than what we have available now. Especially for International payments.

Indeed governments all around the world are on the cusp of potentially employing it's technology with CBDCs – Central Bank Digital Currencies.

Central Bank Digital Currencies (CBDCs)

Nearly all countries now are developing their own CBDC. Australia's is due to launch this year. UK has one in the pipeline dubbed as 'Britcoin.' US has a Federal Payments system called Fed Now on the horizon. Some people believe this is a pre-cursor to their own CBDC.

China released their Digital Yuan just before the Olympics last year. There are many more.

As the name suggests, this type digital currency will be controlled by the central bank of a country.

This is very different to Bitcoin which is an opensource and decentralized blockchain network. With Bitcoin the code is open for anyone to see. It can be changed if and only if the community votes to do so. The miners are incentivised to run the blockchain with rewards.

A CBDC will not be an incentivised network. It may well be a 'cryptocurrency' using a blockchain. However, if so, it will be a 'Permissioned network' i.e. not decentralised and will be accessible only to those with permission.

The code will likely not be opensource for anyone to see.

Within the crypto community the general consensus is that they will be a terrible thing. This is because they are a threat to Bitcoin yet also they are the antithesis of what Bitcoin and decentralization represents.

They are often referred to as 'Spy Coins.' People suggest that because the currency is essentially 'programmable money' that the central banks / governments will be able to control what you can and can't do with your money. And when.

This may well be true. Now no-one can say that this is what governments will actually do, but the ability will be there. It will only take one leader at some point in the future to decide they want control and then they can do what they want. Or worse, as some say, a crisis of some sort may even force a government or Central Bank's hand so that they feel they need to control people's money out of necessity – an unexpected disaster or virus or something...

Taxes and fines could just be taken from your Digital Wallet automatically. Some may say this is efficient. Others disagree and feel that it is someone's right to distribute their own money as and when they want.

I read that Nigeria recently introduced their CBDC but that many in the country were very afraid to use it due to the potential seizure and control of their money. Many Nigerians eventually turned to BTC. Indeed Bitcoin was trading at a premium in Nigeria for a time. I believe it was trading at over $30,000 on Nigerian exchanges while the rest of the global market has seen BTC between $20,000 and $27,000 since February.

So there you have CBDCs in a nutshell. Potential for efficiency and cost saving yet also potential for complete control over your money.

Will this inadvertently lead people to have some Bitcoin as a hedge? Will this cause Bitcoin to be outlawed in many lands? Who knows.

CBDCs will possibly employ blockchain technology and therefore actually be a 'cryptocurrency.'

"Operation Chokepoint 2.0"

The name "Operation Chokepoint 2.0" was coined by someone on twitter for the current US crackdown on cryptocurrency.

So far this year, in 2023, the following events have happened in quick succession:

The crypto exchange Kraken was fined $30 million and ordered by the SEC (Securities and Exchange Commission in the US) to shut down permanently its Staking service.

The crypto exchange Coinbase has been issued a 'Wells Notice' which means the SEC intends to sue it. Coinbase has said it does not know what for as the Wells Notice does not specify. Coinbase intends to take this all the way through courts and defend itself.

Binance US is being sued by the Commodity Futures Trading Commission (CFTC) in the US for violating US trading laws.

The stablecoin BUSD had been ordered to close down and not to issue anymore new stablecoins. As such it is winding down it's stablecoin gradually over the coming months and years.

Signature Bank has gone into liquidation yet the crypto arm of their business was not allowed to be revived. This served as a 247 source for people to convert dollars into crypto and therefore funded a lot of crypto trading. This is a bit of a speculative addition to the "Operation Chokepoint 2.0", however when you list everything together one can be forgiven for being suspicious.

In the UK Natwest has announced it is limiting transfers to Crypto Exchanges to £1000 per day and a maximum of £5000 per month. For consumer protection of course.

In the UK I can no longer transfer funds onto Binance due to it's payment provider removing this facility

Elizabeth Warren in the US has announced she is developing an 'Anti-Crypto Army' to get rid of it.

So as you can see, coordinated or not, crypto is being hit hard with fines and regulations in the US especially. Access to markets are being blocked or reduced in the US and the UK. Services within the crypto exchanges are being disabled and challenged.

Now I only consider myself to have been in this space properly since the end of 2021. There's a common used term called FUD – Fear, Uncertainty and Doubt. I get the impression that this sort of narrative of regulatory overhang and doom is just normal in crypto. Some of the OGs in the space just shrug this sort of thing off as normal. So I find myself comforted by this despite all the negative news pertaining to crypto. However this current situation does feel rather severe.

The mini-banking crisis in the US in early March actually saw Bitcoin rise in value. In theory this was what Bitcoin was made for and born out of. Hence Satoshi Nakamoto's reference to the Times headline in the genesis block – 'Chancellor on the brink of second bail out of the banks.'

On March 13th when Silicon Valley Bank was reported to have problems, BTC was trading around $22,000. A month later it was trading at $28,000. Perhaps there were some people who moved into BTC for safety or comfort from traditional finance, as a hedge in case their money was not safe. Many in the crypto space believe this, though this would be what they want to perceive of course. It's distinctly possible that much of the crypto community just flipped their crypto holdings into BTC rather than people not already in crypto diving into BTC all of a sudden. Although you may ask why would this drive the price as much as it has done and also reportedly lead to the creation of 1 million new BTC wallets? Perhaps there was more to it than just current crypto investors moving to BTC for safety.

As for the regulatory uncertainty surrounding crypto at present, I think regulation would be a good thing as it would clear up some issues once and for all in theory. It seems to me that in the US the exchanges such as Coinbase and Kraken are being a bit naughty and stretching the rules, yet also that the SEC are also refusing to give clear guidelines as to what can and can't be done. Coinbase and Kraken are adamant that they are in constant communication with the SEC but that the SEC never give any real guidance. And now they have been hit with lawsuits for how they are operating.

Perhaps the biggest and most significant debate in the US is whether cryptocurrencies and which ones should be classified as 'Securities'.

I have not studied the US securities and commodities laws, definitions and history extensively but I sort of get a feel that cryptocurrency is a brand new type of asset that just doesn't perhaps fall neatly into any box that already exists in the regulatory framework. You have some people calling some cryptos 'Securities' and other people calling them 'Commodities.'

I gather securities are where you expect an investment to increase in value based on work done by someone else – i.e. the crypto project such as Ethereum in this case.

Granted investors such as myself are buying ETH and awaiting an appreciation in value. This Definitely suggests ETH is a security.

However if I partake in DeFi and need ETH for fees to move around some assets on the blockchain then ETH is behaving as a commodity is it not?

This is a fairly simplistic view and I know it is a lot more complicated than this. For example whether a cryptocurrency project was launched with an 'Initial Share or Coin Offering' (ISO or ICO) is also a factor which contributes to the definition of a product as a security (Ethereum did have an ICO for ETH which ticks a box as a security). However in broad brush strokes, based on what I have gleaned and some common sense that's what I see – it works a bit as both and perhaps therefore is not definitively either a security or a commodity.

Positive Takes on the State of Crypto !
Bitcoin Adoption

Nevertheless, amid all of this, Bitcoin Adoption is just growing. The amount of Bitcoin wallets continues to grow. The Bitcoin network hashrate is at all time highs. The hashrate is a representation of the computational power on the bitcoin network that is mining and competing to earn the Bitcoin block reward as well as the transaction fees.

Bitcoin's strength, security and worth is in it's network and adoption. Bitcoin just continues to do it's thing, block after block with zero downtime and still no successful hacks to the network.

The number of Bitcoin wallet addresses keeps on increasing.

Two potential significant factors in Bitcoin adoption are the Lightning Network and a recent emergence of Bitcoin Ordinals.

The Lightning Network is a Layer 2 scaling solution for the Bitcoin blockchain. This is an attempt to scale the network and it gives near instant payments at far reduced cost. To appreciate this you need to understand that Bitcoin as a base layer (Layer 1 blockchain) is not an especially fast payment system. It operates at about 7 transactions per second. However it is extremely secure. The Lightning Network is aiming to improve this speed and scale the Bitcoin network.

Bitcion Ordinals

The Bitcoin Network has been a victim of it's own success here really. Other, more recently developed blockchains such as Solana can settle transactions at a much higher rate. Solana shows 4,000 TPS as a recent average.[50]

Bitcoin Ordinals are much like NFTs on Bitcoin. So a trend has emerged for people to inscribe individual Satoshis (that is 1 / 100, 000,000[th] of a BTC or 0.000000001 BTC). So some individual Satoshis or 'Sats' are being inscribed with imagery, comments or other things and are being traded as 'Ordinals.' For now it has caught on and is increasing transaction volume and fees on the Bitcoin network. We'll have to see where this goes over time.

On chain data from Glassnode shows that Bitcoin holders are just holding for the long term[51]. People are buying into it as a store of value.

Bitcoin as 'Digital Gold'

The idea of Bitcoin being Digital Gold is the same as the whole 'Store of Value' thesis.

There are similarities if you compare Bitcoin and gold.

For example they are both mined, albeit quite differently but the concept remains that effort is required to produce them both. This is of course by design with Bitcoin.

They are both scarce assets as well. Gold can not be found just anywhere. Bitcoin has a capped supply of 21 million Bitcoins that will never change.

---

[50] Explorer.solana.com
[51] https://insights.glassnode.com/ - Glassnode analyses what is known as 'On Chain Data.' This is basically activity on the blockchain (especially the Bitcoin blockchain) including transaction volume, sizes, values. It can work out how long coins are remaining in the same wallets, the age of coins that are moving. There is so much analysis of the transaction activity and this gives great indicators of investor or 'Hodler' behaviour.

As a store of value, Bitcoin's greatest asset is this hard capped supply. It is becoming very scarce. The inflation rate is around 1.8% at present and this is only going down with each Bitcoin Halving. 91% of Bitcoin is in circulation right now. That leaves 9% new Bitcoin left over the next 100 years! So naturally if demand for BTC stays the same or increases as the technology is adopted then the value will go up. This is fairly easy to deduce. I think cryptocurrency adoption is currently at about 6% of the global population. So we are still early in the adoption timeline. If we assume that adoption will increase then the value of Bitcoin should just go up.

When you couple this with the inflation rate of world currencies like the US dollar for example, you can see how BTC will mathematically increase in value. If the BTC inflation rate will be below 1% from 2024, US dollar inflation will be upwards of this for sure – the US and UK have a 2% annual inflation target[52]. There will be more dollars chasing relatively less Bitcoin, therefore maths just says the price will go up in dollar terms.

One of the arguments for increasing adoption is just the growth of a Digital Generation. As time goes on the older participants of society will be replaced with more digitally native people who are much more likely to adopt something like Bitcoin. One day there may even be Bitcoin friendly world leaders.

Wealth Transfer

As it stands the majority of the world's wealth is held in the population aged 60 and over. This wealth will filter down to the younger generations as time goes on.

Are the younger generation likely to invest in property, shares, bonds, gold or digital assets such as Bitcoin?

---

[52] Among others, James from Invest Answers (youtube.com/investanswers) and Guy from the Coin Bureau (https://www.youtube.com/coinbureau) study and convey this regularly. For example the US and UK governments aim for a 2% annual inflation target however in reality it is invariably significantly more than this.

If you think that the incumbent generation (i.e. those that will inherit the wealth) will allocate more to digital assets than the previous generation then you probably have to conclude that Bitcoin will increase in value. This is a very crude analysis but I believe it has some rationale to it. Time will tell.

General 'Mainstream' Adoption for Cryptocurrencies and NFTs

Other cryptocurrencies are growing their networks. New partnerships are being made all the time – I read the other day that Starbucks in the US are now trialling their rewards as NFTs on the Polygon network. Polygon has also partnered with Disney and many other firms. Ticketmaster are exploring issuing tickets as NFTs. I read that Microsoft is building a crypto browser wallet into is next Microsoft Edge browser version. Flux are making new partnerships constantly. I read that Amazon are exploring creating an NFT marketplace.

Visa, Mastercard and Google are growing their connections to the crypto space.

The list just goes on and on. So the technology is becoming more and more widespread and adopted.

NFTs

Non Fungible Tokens (NFTs) are more complex than meets the eye. Their explosion on the scene was what was perceived as a 'digital J-peg.' An image that someone could buy and use as their Profile picture on various websites. NFTs were changing hands for millions. It was a playground for the rich. Hollywood stars and music stars were buying Bored Ape Yacht Club NFTs for millions. Either as an investment or just to try to be fashionable.

The value of these has since dropped dramatically. Most certainly many are well out of pocket with them as investments for now. Hence the NFT space has had some bad press since all the hype led to money being lost by speculative investors.

They are actually much more than a 'digital J-peg', though they can be used simply as this as digital art. However they are built on blockchain technology and are coded to hold information and can even be coded with smart contracts that enable commissions or royalties to be paid to previous owners.

For example an NFT could be a work of digital art that an artist has produced. They could code the NFT so that they receive a 5% commission or 'royalty' every time that NFT is sold onto another wallet for a fee. Thus this is enabling artists to passively acquire income for their work, without any dispute over the authenticity of their work. It is all coded into the NFT and the transaction history is held on an immutable blockchain ledger.

So as a technology there are many uses-cases to come for NFTs. Indeed via ticketmaster many people could end up using NFTs as tickets while totally unaware that they are based on blockchain technology and unaware that fees are paid in cryptocurrency to move them around from owner to owner (or wallet to wallet).

I heard someone say that blockchain and crypto will 'become mainstream' when millions of people are using it without even realising they are using it.

This is potentially the way this happens.

Yield Nodes NFT

I touched earlier on the Yield Nodes DeFi project that I dabbled with which went to the wall and became illiquid. To their credit they are working hard to turn things around and I believe they are genuine. But this does not mean they will succeed.

However the point of interest here is that they are changing the way your funds are held and investors will soon hold an NFT which represents the funds that you have in the project as well as the yield entitlement. So they are offering 5% per quarter as a yield (that's every 3 months). So I will very soon receive an NFT on the Polygon Network that I can trade if I want to.

The NFT is coded so that the holder is entitled to the yield which increases the value of the NFT once yield is paid out each quarter. So I will soon be able to sell this yield bearing NFT on an open NFT marketplace such as OpenSea. I will try to sell this as soon as I receive it I think. If I can slice it up in any way and keep half and sell half of it as an NFT I may well do so. This will only be to go through a) the process of selling an NFT and b) to hold on to a yield bearing NFT to see how it works. So for educational purposes really.

This use-case where they can have a tradeable value and also the potential use cases I have just touched upon are extremely interesting and have huge potential.

Crypto as an alternative Payment System

In 2022 here are a few examples I came across of crypto being used when traditional payment rails were not available.

Firstly, in Canada there was a truckers strike against the government's Covid 19 restrictions. The government fought against this by freezing the bank accounts of the truckers partaking in the strike. In answer to this a wealthy individual arranged for each trucker to be given a Bitcoin hard wallet with instructions on how to use it to get some funds for their families. I believe there was also some BTC on the wallets provided as well. So essentially someone was giving then an alternative payments system that they could not be frozen out of in order to provide for their family.

Secondly, Russia is rumoured to have used cryptocurrency since it was banned from the SWIFT global banking system at the onset of the Ukraine conflict. This has not necessarily been proven that I can find. However the point is that it is an alternative payment system that works perfectly well. If for any reason you are blocked out of the banking system, either accidentally or due to particular activity, then crypto is an indiscriminate way that you can move money around the world. In most cases when sending funds internationally it's cheaper and faster as well.

Thirdly, I have come across multiple stories of people sending funds home to countries in Africa for example using cryptocurrency. Many people in Africa have no bank accounts and so transferring funds can be difficult, expensive and cumbersome. However with just a mobile phone, crypto was a way that this could be done seamlessly.

How it is redeemed at the other end will depend how cryptocurrency is used and traded locally of course. Nevertheless, the use case is there for people not involved in the traditional banking system, notably in non first world countries.

Summary of the State of Crypto in 2023

As I have discussed Crypto is fresh on the back of a terrible year of price action and bad news stories and outright fraud.

The ever-present issue of money laundering and illicit activity is still hanging over the space.

Nevertheless the technology is potentially about to be employed by some governments worldwide as CBDCs roll out.

So the conclusion has to be that the technology is remarkable and could potentially replace some of the current system in due course, starting with CBDCs. This therefore makes the technology potentially revolutionary, however it arrives.

The cryptocurrency markets and projects themselves appear to be a real problem for governments and regulators. The regulatory framework in the US especially is unclear and not yet mature for this asset class.

Governments in general appear to be restricting access to invest in these Digital Assets. However there is still some positivity coming from Hong Kong (via China) as well as Dubai with regard crypto adoption and even mainland Europe has recently issued some regulatory framework for cryptocurrencies with its 'Markets in Crypto Assets' (MiCA) guidelines.

Bitcoin itself just continues on and gains adoption. Higher hash rate, more users, more wallets. More Hodlers. It is well positioned to become a store of value asset as it grows.

For investors crypto is still hugely volatile and exposed to the potential wrath of regulators and governments.

With the rate at which the crypto space and markets move I'm sure there'll be a lot more action in 2023!

Part 5: My Strategy Moving Forward

In this Part I will outline my current portfolio. I will also discuss my plans as a crypto investor and participant moving forward.

My Current Portfolio

Bitcoin - 70%

Ethereum – 11%

Flux – 5%

Presearch - 5%

Solana - 7%

Cardano - 1%

Cosmos – 1%

I also have a small amount floating around in DeFi, some of the above ETH is on GMX and some very minor amounts of crypto elsewhere - none are significant. Plus whatever comes of the Yield Nodes NFT.

Strategy for 2023 and Beyond

So my portfolio has changed quite radically since my first Coinbase purchases! It is now very heavy BTC and ETH (81% in total). Flux is probably too high a percentage of the portfolio given that it is such a low cap start up and therefore very high risk. However I'm not uncomfortable with this. Similarly Presearch also is probably too high a percentage but this has been due to the rewards I have gained as I have ran nodes for almost a year now.

Again I'm not uncomfortable with this for now. I intend to use some of these rewards to buy more ETH or BTC.

My portfolio can be broken down as:

BTC and ETH heavy at 81%

Alternative Layer 1 blockchains – Solana, Cardano

Cross Chain Protocol - Cosmos

Flux and Presearch – Node rewarding projects where I am participating in the Network

I am generally happy with my portfolio allocations.

My plan for my portfolio development over 2023 is:

1) Gradually add more BTC throughout 2023. My target buying-price range was $17,000 - $21,500. As I write the price is above this and so I am not buying. Should the price show no inclination to go to these levels, then I will begin to add at slightly higher levels from about June/July onwards. However I do not intend to buy above $30,000/$35,000.
2) Add some more ETH. My price target here is at or below $1200. I think this is optimistic, however my main target is BTC. More ETH is a bonus. Again if this price target shows no sign of coming I may adjust and add some at a slightly higher price from June/July onwards. However BTC will take priority.
3) Continue to evolve my Flux Node position with any nodes I can get online myself to earn rewards. May add to my position if the price gets below 0.50 cents.
4) Presearch – keep building up the rewards and add new nodes if I can. Perhaps trade into some more ETH/BTC with some PRE.

5) Remainder of portfolio – Hold onto all other coins. Perhaps stake some to increase my position. I am currently adding some more Solana around the $20 dollar range. I feel this is very undervalued relative to other cryptos right now.

I am prepared for an up and down crypto market in 2023. Why would I expect anything else!? That's how it always is. My point though is that I plan to hold on to it all and add through any downtrends.

I figure that since I have joined the space near the top in 2021 and got this far, the obvious play now is to hang on until the Bitcoin halving cycle and see if any price appreciation ensues.

Things can change quickly though and so if anything drastic happens I may need to re-think. We will see.

Strategy for 2024 and beyond

The potential scenarios I see over the next couple of years are:

1) Halving follows normal pattern leading to new All Time Highs in 2024 and 2025
2) People 'Front run' the halving – i.e. Bitcoin is more mature and more people are setting up for this potential 'trade' around the BTC halving. Therefore the markets front run and an All Time High is lower than expected and comes earlier than previous cycles
3) Halving does not follow normal price appreciation due to global economic factors and or negative crypto regulation

In scenarios 1 and 2 there will be chances to take some profits and hold onto some BTC and other cryptocurrency for the long term.

Scenario 1 looks very possible right now. Global interest rates are high, recessions are either here or looming which may bring rate cuts in 2024 /2025. This will increase Global Liquidity and in theory will fuel asset prices. It is potentially a perfect storm for the Bitcoin Halving.

However! This all seems to good to be true. Expect the unexpected. Nothing is that easy!

Even if interest rates do come down and in turn increase liquidity there could well be an unforeseen factor affecting the markets. The world is quite an interconnected and volatile place right now in my opinion. So we will see.

So if we assume a positive scenario (1 or 2), and this leads to All Time High prices for BTC then the question becomes what do I intend to sell and what do I hold for the long term?

First I need to explain my opinion on where we are with crypto and blockchain as a technology.

My outlook for crypto investing is that these investments are very speculative. They are not guaranteed for any success at all. While use cases are there, adoption of their uses needs to take place for their value to be completely realised. This is because the use-case will drive actual buying and holding demand for the cryptocurrency in question thus accruing significant value to the cryptocurrency.

I do not see that many crypto projects and their cryptocurrencies are that close to their end use case and significant adoption. My best guess is that if Ethereum or Solana are going to be a genuine payment rail for any kind of banking or commercial / retail payment systems (or stock exchange) then we are a few years off.

Similarly the Flux concept and network is growing and they are adding new business users to their platform as well as partnering with many large entities as well. However their growth as a business is not that significant just yet. Again, if they are to be successful, they are a few years away from actual true demand for the Flux token taking over it's value and driving the price of the token up and up to reward early investors.

My point here is that whatever comes in the aftermath of the next BTC cycle in terms of price appreciation across the board in cryptocurrencies, it will likely still only be speculation from investors rather than genuine demand for the cryptocurrency itself.

And therefore my decisions on what to hold on to and for how long actually depends as much on my long term belief as well how much profit I would like to take if the prices do appreciate.

So below is my working thesis and how I see things:

Bitcoin

I see Bitcoin as both a long term investment as well as the potential for mid-term profits – i.e. 2024/2025

My working estimate for the post halving price range is $75,000 - $250,000 in this next cycle. This is speculation and no-one has any more insight than anyone else. You may try to verify or gauge opinion on whether this price range is likely but please realise that it is all speculation and nobody knows what's round the corner. It may stay around $20,000 - $30,000 for 10 years !!

The fact is I invest in and hold BTC because I believe the price will go up. Those who don't invest clearly believe the price will not go up. That is fine. I am a BTC investor and therefore I am positioned for this next cycle to play out.

The sensible thing to me seems to be to layer out from $65,000 and upwards. $65,000 is around the previous cycle All Time High ($64,000 April 2021 and $67,000 November 2021)[53]

My plan is to sell half of my BTC holding and HODL on to the other half for the longer term appreciation.

So if I sell 50% of my BTC I am proposing to do so at the following levels:

$65,000 – sell 10%

$75,000 – sell 10%

$95,000 (front running the psychological $100,000) – sell 10%

$100,000 – sell 10%

$120,000 – sell 10%

If the price goes any higher than this ... well brilliant. I will probably be tempted to sell some more!

I've heard from people who were around and in profit in previous cycles, and they say it gets hard to sell your BTC when the price just keeps going up. It's so easy to just keep holding and get greedy in case it is going higher than you think. But of course the market can so quickly reverse and you have then missed your chance!

So let's see if I can heed the advice and stick to my plan above! I'll perhaps let you know how it goes down the line. Hopefully it actually plays out with prices at these levels!

---

[53] There was a 'Double Top' in the previous cycle high in 2021. This is where the price chart peaked twice around the same level in April and then in November 2021

Market Top Indicators

Another factor which will affect my decisions when this time comes is some 'Market Top' indicators that can be used.

'Glassnode' and Ben Cowen's 'Into the Cryptoverse' websites and YouTube channels showcase some tools and metrics that they monitor which have historically been good indicators of market trends and when they are likely to change.[54]

2 examples are social activity and BTC transaction fees.

Social Activity is a chart I have come across from 'Into the Cryptoverse' that indicates when Bitcoin and crypto is being widely talked about on social media – twitter, facebook and others. It also tracks the volume of new subscribers to crypto YouTube and Twitter channels

So if these metrics indicate that Bitcoin and crypto is a hot topic then this indicates high interest in crypto and therefore that the market may be nearing a top. This is because increased social discussion has previously been an indicator of increased demand for BTC which in turn increases it's price.

Of course you never know where the top of a cycle will be just like we are right now guessing where the bottom of this cycle is. Has it already passed? Nevertheless indicators such as these social indicators can help. Previous cycle data has shown this correlation.

BTC transaction fees are reported by Glassnode (among others) and indicate the amount of on chain activity on the Bitcoin network. Transaction fees will be higher with more activity, as users will pay more to have their transaction processed more quickly if there is a lot of traffic on the network. When crypto and BTC is a hot topic and users are coming in, fees can spike and this

---

[54] Intothecryptoverse.com and youtube.com/@intothecryptoverse
Also glassnode.com and youtube.com/glassnode

can be an indicator that the market can be near the top of the cycle. This is again because increased activity means demand for BTC and therefore usually higher prices.

These are 2 of the factors I will consider on top of my price targets if the scenario of All Time High's plays out after the halving. This is just to get an indication of when the market may be around the top of the cycle.

Other very useful indicators include the **Puell Multiple** chart and the **Pi Cycle Top** indicator.[55]

Note on all non-BTC holdings:

All of my holdings, but less so BTC, are particularly vulnerable right now to regulation from around the world. Especially in the USA. The US are threatening to label all cryptocurrencies except BTC as 'securities' which may mean they become unavailable on many US exchanges and potentially illegal for US citizens to hold as investments.

This could potentially cause their prices to drop significantly at any time.

So when I said I plan to hold on to everything in 2023 unless anything drastic happens – this could be one of those things.

So my below comments/plans assume that this does not happen in the meantime! If it does I may decide to sell some of these cryptos. It is much less likely that I will sell my BTC due to regulations.

---

[55] Again I have become familiar with these charts from Glassnode. Worth being aware of these as a BTC and crypto investor.

Ethereum

As far as ETH goes I believe this also a good long term investment as well as an investment for mid-term profits in the next cycle.

Similarly I plan to sell half of my ETH and HODL the other 50% of my investment for the long term.

As I have previously mentioned the BTC price generally leads the whole crypto market and the other cryptocurrencies just follow in it's wake and can even move up or down faster than BTC.

Sometimes BTC runs off on it's own and the altcoins follow after a while. Historically this 'while' or delay in the altcoin appreciation after a BTC increase, can be days, weeks or months. So it is very hard to gauge when is the actual best time to begin sell.

I do separate Ethereum from the other altcoins as a much safer and more stable investment or 'bet.'

Therefore my timeframe for starting to layer out of Ethereum is more or less in line with the time frame for starting to sell BTC. So my sell points for ETH in particular is less tied to it's USD price but more tied to the timing of BTC hitting it's highs and my price targets for BTC previously mentioned.

I do not believe this is the perfect strategy, however I haven't currently got a better one.

One thing I have been exposed to is the price of ETH relative to BTC rather than just considering each crypto relative to it's USD price.

Since 2021 ETH has typically fluctuated between 0.06 and 0.08 BTC. See Figure 5.

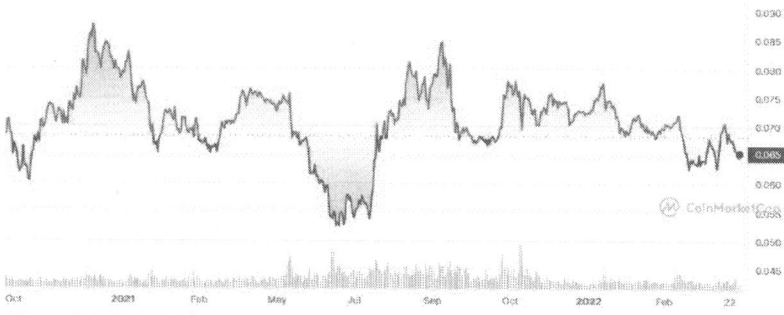

Figure 5. ETH BTC Chart October 2021 - April 2023. Source Coinmarketcap.com[56]

So if we use this range to decide when to trade in and out of ETH you could argue that to check the ETH/BTC valuation when BTC is at $65,000 would dictate whether ETH is a 'sell' or not at this point.

If BTC is $65,000 and ETH is sitting at 0.065BTC, then I may decide to hold on for while. But then what if BTC just plummets in USD terms and ETH stays the same in USD terms? – ETH could then be at 0.08 BTC yet the same USD price.

With this in mind I guess how you trade this information it depends on whether your goal is to acquire BTC or ETH or USD. For the purpose of this section I am referring to profit taking in USD terms. Therefore the ETH/USD price is ultimately what matters to me at this point.

Therefore I will probably have the same strategy and begin to layer out of ETH when BTC gets to $65,000. And from there I guess I'll see how the ETH/BTC pair is performing to help me gauge how much further ETH could run.

ETH may have more room to run when BTC is at it's high. So I will set my price targets around this time.

Of course there are more factors that just the ETH/BTC price chart. There could be news, adoption stories and all sorts of other things affecting the

---

[56] https://coinmarketcap.com/currencies/ethereum/eth/btc/

price. But for me the BTC/USD price is my first indicator of where the overall market is at.

The fact that I believe ETH is very solid and will still run well when BTC is at or around it's high, means that I can consider ETH sell prices in light of the BTC USD price. I don't feel the same about other altcoins. I feel they are more volatile and need a separate approach.

Solana and Cardano

Solana and Cardano are the only 2 of many Layer 1 projects that I chose to hold. I don't believe anyone knows which layer 1s will end up with the most adoption and therefore the most value accrued.

I picked Solana because they are the cheapest and fastest layer 1 blockchain, they have lots of Daily Active Users – around 200,000 at present.[57] Their team has a strong history in telecomms and they seem a very astute marketing outfit. The Solana phone – Saga – will be released soon. This is a smartphone that is crypto native in that there is a secure crypto wallet built into the phone and access to Dapps will be straightforward.

They had shops in US shopping malls which they have recently closed. However the intention to connect with the general public was a good one in my view.

However this does not mean they will be adopted. But they have a good chance.

As for Cardano I hold some of this I guess because they seem to be continually developing their number of Dapps on the network, they have added their own stablecoins recently, they are getting around the world and appear to be making partnerships in order to develop use-cases for their blockchain. There is seldom any bad press so to speak around their team.

---

[57] Data from tokenterminal.com April 2023 –
https://tokenterminal.com/terminal/projects/solana

They definitely have the 'slow and steady' approach. To me they seem very genuine and open about everything.

However you could equally say similar things about many other layer 1 blockchains and teams that I have not invested in. Avalanche, Algorand etc. I have no more insight than other general investors as to which will survive and thrive in the Layer 1 race.

So these I see as speculative investments and as such am happy to take some profits yet also hold some for the long term as well.

Price targets I have an eye on for Solana

$100

$150

$250

$500 and $1000 if it really takes off long term.

My average cost price for my Solana holdings is around $60. This has taken such a hit due to the FTX crash.

My working thesis is that it could hit around $150 - $200 if there is a bull run after the Bitcoin halving.

If Solana does succeed long term (5+ years) then I believe $500 to $1000 are in play.

I am currently inclined to hold on to my Solana long term but I will be ready to move if something does happen or if the price gets up to the $200 + levels. I will then likely layer out some of my holdings from here. And if I stake my Solana I will not be staking all of it! Maximum 50% I reckon!

I will be keeping tabs on the project development.

My cost basis for Cardano is $0.50

This is a very small part of my portfolio.

I have an eye on $1.50 to begin layering out of this one. I will likely sell 50% - 75% of this on the way up to $3 which is the previous all time high for Cardano.

This may change if any news suggests Cardano will be even better positioned for the longer term. Again at this point no-one knows who the outstanding Layer 1 will be in time. So I'll hang on to some just in case.

Flux

I'm very keen on Flux as a project as you may have picked up, I just like what it represents and the opportunity it presents for the average person to get involved.

I want to hold onto some of this and see how the project develops long term. There's a website called Bunny Analyst which analyses the throughput of users and subscribers to the Flux network and also statistics like how many customers are using the Flux cloud services.[58]

So I intend to watch this carefully to monitor the growth and adoption.

I have long term prices in mind of $5 and $10 for Flux. However my decision whether to hold or sell will depend entirely on the growth and adoption of the network. I think this could be a nugget down the line and I want to hold some if not all for the long term. Also to run nodes I need to hold the collateral and so I will need to hold onto some as long as I am running some nodes.

I will likely sell some around the $3 price level and if the price does get up and around $5 then perhaps I'll sell some more. Again I may sell here with a view to buying back if the price ever dips back to the $1- $3 level.

---

[58] Bunnyanalyst.com/flux

Presearch

I think Presearch has long term potential as well but I do intend to sell at least 25-50% of my holdings.

I have a target of $0.50 in mind to begin layering out of some PRE.

I started buying around $0.20. My average price will be around $0.07 I'd say, if I take into account my node rewards as well.

I may take some profit off the table at $0.20 depending on what stage of the market is at if the price ever gets back as far as $0.20! And any movements above here will perhaps encourage me to take some more profits off the table as well.

I think the narrative of Presearch and the rewards programme for the network is again a very good idea. It's a project that the average investor can fully understand and invest accordingly to earn whatever small income they can.

The narrative around people's data and privacy could easily cause a project like Presearch to gain in popularity very rapidly and almost out of nowhere. I don't for a minute consider it a threat to Google but just a bit of market share will mean a lot for the project and the value of the token.

What I do also like about Presearch is part of the tokenomics. If someone wants to advertise on the search engine they 'Stake' PRE as a 'bid' on a keyword. So to advertise on 'Buy Bitcoin' for example you need to buy and stake – i.e. lock up – some PRE to come up in the search results. This is great for PRE as it is creating 'buy and hold' demand for the token. This will push up the price of the token.

However my concerns revolve around some other tokenomics of Presearch. There is a max supply of 500 million PRE.[59]

Coin Market Cap states that there are 397 million in circulating supply.

Nodes are rewarded with approx. 3.5 PRE per day. There are approx. 80,000 nodes on the network.

So if 80,000 nodes are earning approx. 3.5 PRE per day then that is a total of 280,000 PRE per day paid out in rewards.

In one year that is 365 x 280,000 is approx. 100 million PRE.

So in theory the remaining 100 million PRE will be paid out over the next year. This is on the assumption that the remaining PRE that are not in circulation (approx. 103 million) constitute the reward pool from which the Node rewards are paid.

Either way 20% of total circulation as it stands will be paid out in rewards in the next year.

That's NOT a good inflation rate!

I asked the question to the Presearach founder, Colin Pape, in one of the weekly Presearch YouTube videos and he suggested rewards could eventually be paid in another token other than PRE, or that there could be some form of buy back where the Presearch entity buys back PRE on the open market. Neither option was suggested with any certainty.

The real positive is the theoretical scarcity of the PRE token. If all 500 million PRE are in circulation in a couple of years then that's definitely a driver for price appreciation.

---

[59] Data from Coin Market Cap - March 2023 - https://coinmarketcap.com/currencies/presearch/

So I'm interested to see which way the project goes with this. I trust the team and the founder Colin Pape. The decision on this though will directly affect the future value of the PRE token whatever decision is made on this topic.

Ultimately the 'team' leading the project will leave such decisions to the Presearch community. However at this stage in it's development it has not got as far as this. Therefore some decisions are still 'centralized' for the time being.

I suppose it's possible that the PRE token becomes some sort of governance token which gives holders voting rights on decisions exactly like this one on tokenomics. If this does happen I'm not sure that gives great value appreciation potential to the PRE token. Anyway, time will tell.

Cosmos

My current plan is to sell all of my Cosmos at $26 and above.

This is my average cost price. I would have sold my Cosmos before now around the FTX collapse – however it was staked and the unlock period was about 10 or 20 days and by the time it as unlocked the price had dropped so far I figured I would hold onto it until better times!

Cosmos is actually getting some good press and may have a bright future as a cross chain protocol. However the staking reward is around 17% - 20% and so this inflation puts me off. Likewise many of the transactions on the blockchain are almost free and so minimal profit is made in fees by the protocol and therefore fees are not a demand driver for the Cosmos currency. So I bought into this before really realising this (lesson learned).

The community made a proposal to change the tokenomics recently but it was not accepted. I forget the details but I believe this would have improved these tokenomics of the currency.

So for this reason I don't maintain a great allegiance and the inflation rate is very high. It is a very small part of my portfolio anyway. Nevertheless I'll check in on the progress and any tokenomics changes before letting go just in case!

I will likely re-stake and earn the extra coins in the meantime.

So the above is my strategy for in case the market heats up after the Bitcoin halving in 2024. Some elements of my strategy are fairly decisive and some elements of it are dependant on how things evolve either for individual projects or for the market in general.

In this case, as outlined above, my planned amount to sell equates to around 50% of my portfolio. This of course leaves me with 50% to see where it all goes long term. I could well decide to buy back some of the BTC and ETH that I eventually sell, if and when the price pulls back after the market top has hit.

Equally I may well decide to sell more than 50% of my crypto portfolio. You need a plan when investing but you have to be willing to change your thesis quickly and react accordingly to any changes in circumstances. Crypto is just so volatile and fast moving that I am aware that this could happen.

If there are no new All Time Highs for BTC and many (or any) of these cryptocurrencies then I will just assess the reasons for this and decide how to act accordingly. If this is due to economic factors then my inclination would be to hold onto it all and be patient.

If cryptocurrency is suffering some pressure in terms of regulation then I will make my decisions for each cryptocurrency on an individual basis. I suspect any regulation would not affect BTC too much but may decimate the altcoin space. I may flip everything into BTC in this case. We will see.

Lesson from Current Bear Market

One factor I should highlight at this point is that the above strategy involves me holding on to some altcoins after the next potential bull market.

As per the sections earlier in this book, holding onto anything in a bear market is likely going to mean that the $ value of the portfolio will suffer severely. I found that BTC and ETH were the best crypto assets to hold in a downtrend. So in theory if I learn from my initial experience I perhaps should cash in all other altcoins near the top of the market and hold BTC and ETH only in the case of another cyclical downtrend after the next halving appreciation.

This is all subject to the cycle behaving similarly to before of course. Though the point is that I need to be prepared for this and decide whether I will flip into BTC and ETH or hold on to some of the others on the way down.

I suppose I will entertain this consideration and see how the market evolves. If PRE and FLUX appreciate a lot then the node rewards are nice to keep coming in either as potential income or simply to build the portfolio if nothing else. It will depend a lot on the progress of the projects and what their trajectory is I suppose.

So I guess while my plan A is to sell roughly half and hold onto half of my crypto, I remain in deliberation of the best 'bear market' strategy, assuming the cycle plays out in a familiar fashion.

But a significant factor just has to be the overall progress of the projects I have invested in. I gather and have seen that so many promising or hyped blockchain projects just come and go from one cycle to the next. With this in mind I need to make sure that I extract at least close to my initial investment in a project in case it does not prosper for another cycle.

As Benjamin Cowen from Into the Cryptoverse states - it's all just dubious speculation in any case!

Summary to Crypto Files 2022

I hope this book has provided some insight into the crypto world, De-fi, the crypto markets and also provided some entertainment as well. 2022 was a very eventful 'bear market' year and so far 2023 has been very eventful as well.

Hopefully being introduced properly to crypto in a bear market and surviving will bode well for me in the future. I certainly feel I've been through a lot in this short time. As have so many others in the space in 2022.

For investors crypto is a very high risk-reward play and is certainly not for the faint hearted. The technology itself is moving fast, gaining users and grabbing attention. The mechanics of the technology is fascinating and learning about it is very mentally stimulating. Equally fascinating is the dynamic of the whole space. It feels like a mix of early adopters, technology 'geeks', high flying Venture Capital, genuine savvy investors, ordinary investors and out and out crooks.

My macro economic education as well as my investing education has been turbo charged. I didn't envision this but feel I have really benefitted in this regard. I just need to apply it accordingly to reap the benefits in the future.

More specifically to crypto, in my first year here are a few things that I believe I have achieved;

I've managed to buy and hold some investments.

I've also learned about decentralised blockchain networks and how to contribute to these blockchain networks and earn the rewards that are available for this.

I've dabbled in some low, medium and high risk DeFi and subsequently both learned some skills and also been burned as well.

I've managed to witness some of the craziest blow ups in crypto history and probably financial history for that matter.

I've 'found Bitcoin' properly I guess. I understand more clearly what it is, how it works, what it represents and what it may become in the future.

And finally I've become quite comfortable transacting in crypto and moving funds around on blockchains.

I did expect a bit of volatility but what I got was above and beyond my expectations. The space remains fascinating and I feel there's more to uncover as I move forward in this journey. As I have said I'll see out this whole Bitcoin cycle and subsequent year or two and see what the lay of the land is as we go. If I've learned anything, it is that you can expect the unexpected in crypto so you need to be on your toes!

To finish with I would just ask that if you've got this far and got something out of the book if you would leave me a review wherever you bought the book from I would appreciate it. With time permitting I intend to continue to write about this topic as it still fascinates me. I will have at least another two years to report in this 'Bitcoin cycle', whatever it brings in the form of events or education. Also there are many other areas of crypto besides that interest me enough to consider trying and giving my take on was well.

Many thanks for your time.

YouTube channels I subscribe to or have previously subscribed to (alphabetical)

Coin Bureau - youtube.com/coinbureau

The Go-To for Crypto content. Any crypto topic has been covered here before. How to guides, In depth analysis on very many coins and projects. Some great general economic news researched as well. A must have. Loves a conspiracy theory too!

Crypto Casey - youtube.com/cryptocasey

Good channel and content. Been in crypto a while and very experienced. Some great educational content.

CTO Larsson - youtube.com/ctolarsson

Former mobile phone developer for Ericsson. A unique flavour and excellent assessment and analytics. A favourite of mine.

Dapp University - youtube.com/dappuniversity

A blockchain developer who's been in the space for a long time. Good to have a developer's insight on many things in crypto. In my view.

Digital Asset News - youtube.com/@DigitalAssetNews

Cool, easy going Crypto OG. Doesn't overvalue himself. Great content. Seen it all before. Steady head in Crypto.

Gareth Soloway - youtube.com/@GarethSolowayProTrader

Experienced trader. Crypto and stocks.

Glassnode - youtube.com/glassnode

Brilliant 'On Chain' Analytics. Can't ignore this channel.

Invest Answers - youtube.com/investanswers

- very analytical. Loves numbers and data. Experienced investor and trader. Brilliant on Macro as well as Crypto analysis.

Into the Cryptoverse – youtube.com/@intothecryptoverse

Excellent Analysis. Crypto OG. Seen it all before and called 2022 perfectly.

Ivan on Tech - youtube.com/ivanontech

Very excitable character. Developer and been in the space a long time. Has great insight and perspective.

Money ZG - youtube.com/moneyzg

Great Analysis. Very level-headed and good analysis.

Paul Barron Network - youtube.com/paulbarronnetwork

American style Crypto news/debating studio. Very sensible and thorough coverage.

Presearch – youtube.com/c/Presearch

Provides weekly updates on the Presearch project. Involves the audience as well by taking questions every week.

Real Vision Finance - youtube.com/realvisionfinance

Macro and Crypto channel. Great overview of the markets in general

Tokenmetrics - youtube.com/tokenmetrics

Founder Ian Balina has made some good money trading crypto with algorithms. Interesting to get his take on how he is trading any market conditions

Your Friend Andy - youtube.com/yourfriendandy

Genuine guy. A bit de-gen/high risk at times. Good entertaining channel.

The above are sources of crypto content and entertainment that I have learned from.

Once again, nothing in this book can be construed as financial or investment advice.

Printed in Great Britain
by Amazon